C000263070

ISLAMIC
TEACHINGS SERIES

Fasting & Spiritual Retreat

ISLAMIC
TEACHINGS SERIES

Fasting & Spiritual Retreat

COMPILED FROM THE WORKS OF
SHAYKH-UL-ISLAM DR
MUHAMMAD TAHIR-UL-QADRI

Minhaj-ul-Quran Publications

Published by Minhaj-ul-Quran Publications
292-296 Romford Road
London, E7 9HD
United Kingdom

First Published December 2011

www.minhajpublications.com

© Minhaj-ul-Quran Publications

All rights reserved. Aside from fair use, meaning a few pages or less for non-profit educational purposes, review, or scholarly citation, no part of this publication may be reproduced, stored in a retrieval system, or transmitted in any form or by any means, electronic, mechanical, photocopying, recording, or otherwise, without the prior written permission of the copyright owner.

ISBN: 978-1-908229-09-0

Typeset: Muhammad Farooq Rana

Acknowledgements:
Mrs Farida Sajjad, Misbah Kabeer, Muhammad Farooq Rana, Muhammad Sohail Siddiqui, Waqas Amin, Rafiq Patel, Asma Parveen, Mariam Khalid, Karim Mamdani and all other brothers and sisters involved in this compilation.

Printed in Turkey by Mega Print,Istanbul

Table of Contents

Foreword

Human beings have been created to worship Allah, and have been prescribed to acquire awareness of and sincerity with Him. Acts of worship, as if they are no more than a habit, may earn you reward in the hereafter but give you no support at all for obtaining awareness and spiritual light. The same acts of worship, when they are performed with true, sincere and acute observation of the divine presence,[1] earn you a station of proximity to and feeling of company with the Lord Almighty, where you receive delightful divine enchantments to enkindle your faith as well as reassurance for your soul's aspirations to a place in the divine court in a state of tranquillity and His good pleasure.[2]

Minhaj-ul-Qur'an International works under the patronage of his eminence, Shaykh-ul-Islam Prof Dr Muhammad Tahir-ul-Qadri and discharges its duties of guiding and uplifting the Muslim Umma at each level.

This book is part of the *Taʿlīmāt Islam* series compiled from the works and lectures of Shaykh-ul-Islam Dr Muhammad Tahir-ul-Qadri. Their aim is to provide readers with both a general overview and where needed, some indepth information and guidance on the basics of

---

[1] The reference is to the hadith of Jibrīl where it says that you should worship Allah as if you were seeing Him.

[2] The reference is to the verse of the Qur'an which says: 'O contented (pleased) self! Return to your Lord in such a state that you are both the aspirant to, and the aspired of, His pleasure (i.e., you seek His pleasure and He seeks yours).' [*al-Fajr*, 89:27–28].

Islam. All of the primary subjects within the three branches of the Shariah, *ʿaqīda* (doctrine), *fiqh* (jurisprudence), *tasawwuf* (spirituality and self purification) are covered and a general basic understanding of Islam in a modern context through an easy to follow question and answer format. Some of the most common yet unanswered day to day issues are replied to using juristic methods from sound sources of Quran and hadith.

These are not only of benefit for the purpose of self study, for anybody of any age and from every walk of life, it is also a very useful reference source which caters for the needs of academic institutions, libraries and study circles.

We pray God Almighty to grant us the best of faith and deeds and accept all the services rendered by all the persons involved in bringing about this collection.

Fasting and Spiritual Retreat

1. The Blessed Month of Ramaḍān

Q.1. What does Ramaḍān mean?

A: The word Ramaḍān, in Arabic, comes from the stem *ramaḍa*, which means 'parchedness and scorching heat'.[3]

The month of fasting is called Ramaḍān because it makes the fasting person feel hunger pangs and raging thirst.

Mullā ʿAlī al-Qārī states that Ramaḍān was derived from *ramḍāʾ*, which means scorched land. For this reason, Ramaḍān would mean 'extremely hot'. When the Arabs picked the names for the months, they named each month according to the time of the year in which it fell and the season it arrived in. They named the month that happened to fall in the scorching hot days, Ramaḍān.[4]

Q.2. What is the importance of Ramaḍān in the light of Qurʾān and hadith?

A. Ramaḍān is the blessed month of the Islamic calendar which is honoured by the descent of the Qurʾān. It was on one of the blessed nights of Ramaḍān when the Qurʾān was revealed to the lowest heaven. It is for this very reason that Allah ﷻ blessed that night above all other

---

[3] Ibn Manẓūr, *Lisān al-ʿArab*, 7:162.

[4] Mullā ʿAlī al-Qārī, *Mirqāt al-Mafātīḥ*, 4:292.

nights and declared it to be the Night of Destiny (*layla al-qadr*). The Qur'ān says:

(لَيْلَةُ ٱلْقَدْرِ خَيْرٌ مِّنْ أَلْفِ شَهْرٍ)

The Night of Destiny is better than a thousand months (in merit of excellence, blessings, reward and recompense).[5]

Here we mention some of the Prophetic traditions regarding the merits of excellence, reward and blessings granted in this month.

Abū Hurayra ؓ reported that the Prophet ﷺ said:

إِذَا دَخَلَ رَمَضَانُ فُتِحَتْ أَبْوَابُ الْجَنَّةِ ، وَغُلِّقَتْ أَبْوَابُ جَهَنَّمَ ،

وَسُلْسِلَتِ الشَّيَاطِينُ.

'When Ramaḍān starts the doors of paradise are opened, those of Hell are closed and devils are chained.'[6]

We can deduce the distinctive honour granted to Ramaḍān from the following hadith which has been reported on the authority of Abū Huraya ؓ:

مَنْ صَامَ رَمَضَانَ إِيَّانًا وَّاحْتِسَابًا، غُفِرَ لَهُ مَا تَقَدَّمَ مِنْ ذَنْبِهِ.

'Whoever fasts the month of Ramaḍān in the state of faith and for the sake of its reward, all his previous sins are forgiven.'[7]

The bliss and felicity carried by all other months cannot match those of a single moment in this month. Abū Hurayra ؓ narrated the words of the Holy Prophet ﷺ:

---

[5] Qur'ān, *al-Qadr*, 97:3.
[6] Narrated by al-Bukhārī in *al-Ṣaḥīḥ*, 3:1194 §3103.
[7] Narrated by al-Bukhārī in *al-Ṣaḥīḥ*, 2:709 §1910.

ـضانَ إِيْمَاناً وَّاحْتِسَاباً، غُفِرَ لَهُ مَا تَقَدَّمَ مِنْ ذَنْبِهِ.

'Whoever stands (in worship) in the m
Ramaḍān in the state of faith and for the
its reward, all his previous sins are forgive

Q.3. How would the Prophet ﷺ welcome Ramaḍān?

A: The love of the Prophet ﷺ towards the month of Ramaḍān can be seen in his frequent prayers to receive it. His vigilant observance for it would always start by fasting strictly during the previous month (namely Shaʿbān). He ﷺ would always receive Ramaḍān with great eagerness and welcome it in high passion and desire for it. He would sometimes ask the Companions ﷺ three times:

مَاذَا يَسْتَقْبِلُكُمْ وَمَاذَا تَسْتَقْبِلُوْنَ؟

'Do you have any idea what receives you and what you are welcoming?'

'Umar b. Al-Khaṭṭāb ﷺ asked if there was some revelation about to descend or some battle about to start. The Prophet's response to both the questions was negative. Then he asked what the matter was! The Prophet ﷺ said:

إِنَّ اللهَ يَغْفِرُ فِي أَوَّلِ لَيْلَةٍ مِنْ شَهْرِ رَمَضَانَ لِكُلِّ أَهْلِ الْقِبْلَةِ.

'Allah forgives all the people of *qibla* on the first night of the month of Ramaḍān.'[9]

---

[8] Narrated by al-Bukhārī in *al-Ṣaḥīḥ*, 1:22 §37.

[9] Narrated by al-Mundhirī in *al-Targhīb wa al-Tarhīb*, 2:64 §1502.

Anas ﵁ reported that the Messenger ﷺ would make the following supplication at the start of the month of Rajab:

اَللّٰهُمَّ بَارِكْ لَنَا فِي رَجَبٍ وَشَعْبَانَ، وَبَارِكْ لَنَا فِي رَمَضَانَ.

> 'O Allah! Bless the month of Rajab and Shaʿbān for us and bless Ramaḍān for us.'[10]

Another narration is as follows:

عَنْ أُسَامَةَ بْنِ زَيْدٍ ﵄ قَالَ: قُلْتُ: يَا رَسُولَ اللهِ ، لَمْ أَرَكَ تَصُوْمُ شَهْراً مِنَ الشُّهُورِ مَا تَصُوْمُ مِنْ شَعْبَانَ؟ قَالَ ﷺ: ذَلِكَ شَهْرٌ يَغْفِلُ النَّاسُ عَنْهُ بَيْنَ رَجَبٍ وَرَمَضَانَ وَهُوَ شَهْرٌ تُرْفَعُ فِيهِ الأَعْمَالُ إِلَى رَبِّ الْعَالَمِينَ، فَأُحِبُّ أَنْ يُرْفَعَ عَمَلِي وَأَنَا صَائِمٌ.

> Usāma b. Zayd ﵄ asked the Prophet ﷺ why he would always fast during the month of Shaʿbān far more than any other month. [Literally: 'I don't see you fast during any month like you do during Shaʿbān.'] The holy Prophet ﷺ replied, 'That is an important month between Rajab and Ramaḍān. People often fall unmindful of it. That is a month when the deeds (of the whole previous year) are raised to the court of Lord of the Universe. I want my deeds to be presented to His court while I am in the state of fasting.'[11]

Umm Salama ﵂, Mother of the Believers, said that she had never seen the Prophet ﷺ fast two consecutive

---

[10] Narrated by Abū Nuʿaym in *Ḥilya al-Awliyāʾ*, 6:269.

[11] Narrated by al-Nasāʾī in *al-Sunan*, 4:201 §2357; and Aḥmad b. Ḥanbal in *al-Musnad*, 5:201 §21801.

months except for Shaʿbān, as he 🌸 would join it with Ramaḍān.[12]

The month of Shaʿbān is like an introduction to Ramaḍān. We must increase the deeds that we perform during Ramaḍān in this month, namely, fasting and reciting the Qurʾān. Ibn Rajab al-Ḥanbalī writes in his book named *Laṭāʾif al-Maʿārif* on page 258:

> The purpose of increasing fasts and reciting the Qurʾān in Shaʿbān is to accomplish the preparations for absorbing the felicities of Ramaḍān, as well as to prepare the lower self to obey the Most Compassionate wholeheartedly.

The practice of the Companions 🌸 also supports this understanding. Anas 🌸 sheds light upon this:

كَانَا الْـمُسْلِمُوْنَ إِذَا دَخَلَ شَعْبَانُ، أَكَبُّوا عَلَى الْـمَصَاحِفِ فَقَرَؤُوْهَا، وَأَخْرَجُوْا زَكَاةَ أَمْوَا لِـهِمْ تَقْوِيَةً لِلضَّعِيْفِ وَالْـمِسْكِينِ عَلَى صِيَامِ رَمَضَانَ.

‘With the start of Shaʿbān, Muslims would incline to reciting the Qurʾān. They would subtract the Zakat applicable to their wealth to help the poor and needy, they would fast and spend their Ramaḍān in ease and peace of mind.’[13]

---

[12] Narrated by al-Nasāʾī in *al-Sunan*, 4:150 §2175.

[13] Narrated by Ibn Rajab al-Ḥanbalī in *Laṭāʾif al-Maʿārif*, p. 258.

Q.4. What was the routine practice of the Prophet ﷺ during Ramaḍān?

A: During the blessed month of Ramaḍān, the acts of worship and spiritual striving would increase a great deal as compared to other days. Awe of the Divine Presence and aspiration to the Divine Court, would rise to a climax and the hours of worship at night would increase. The study of the biography of the holy Prophet ﷺ guides us to the following main points.

Great worship and austerity

Mother of the Believers, ʿĀʾisha ﵂ reports:

كَانَ رَسُولُ اللهِ ﷺ إِذَا دَخَلَ رَمَضَانُ تَغَيَّرَ لَوْنُهُ وَكَثُرَتْ صَلَاتُهُ وَابْتَهَلَ فِي الدُّعَاءِ وَأَشْفَقَ مِنْهُ.

> 'The face of Allah's Messenger ﷺ would change colour (out of awe for Allah) and his prayer would increase with the start of Ramaḍān. He ﷺ would beseech Allah humbly and earnestly and fear him.'[14]

Pre-dawn meal for fasting and fast breaking

The holy Prophet ﷺ would start the fast by having a pre-dawn meal for fasting, towards its later time and he would end his fast with *ifṭār*, eating it at an early time. Anas ﵁ reported the word of the Prophet ﷺ as follows:

تَسَحَّرُوا، فَإِنَّ فِي السُّحُوْرِ بَرَكَةً.

> 'Eat pre-dawn meal for fasting, there is blessing in it.'[15]

---

[14] Narrated by al-Bayhaqī in *Shuʿab al-Īmān*, 3:310 §3625.
[15] Narrated by Muslim in *al-Ṣaḥīḥ*, 2:770 §1095.

Abū Qays reported that ʿAmr b. al-ʿĀs 🙵 narrated the words of the Prophet 🙵 as follows:

> 'The difference between our fast and that of the People of the Book is that of eating pre-dawn meal for fasting.'[16]

NIGHT PRAYER

The Ramaḍān nights of the Prophet 🙵 were full of devotion, offering prayer, glorifying Allah, reciting the Qurʾān and keeping His remembrance. The collective form of prayer known as *tarāwīḥ* is a portion of it. The holy Prophet 🙵 expressed the importance of occupying the nights of Ramaḍān with worship in the following words:

> 'Whoever fasts the days of Ramaḍān and prays at its nights with faith and intention of reward, becomes purified of all sins [he is sinless] like the day he was born.'[17]

ABUNDANCE OF CHARITABLE DEEDS

Giving charity was one of the most manifest features in the life of our beloved Prophet 🙵. His generosity would never turn away anyone in need empty-handed. This generosity would increase remarkably during Ramaḍān as compared to the other eleven months. His natural magnanimity and princely open-handedness would grow beyond all bounds of benevolence. ʿAbd Allah b. ʿAbbās 🙵 narrates:

فَإِذَا لَقِيَهُ جِبْرِيلُ ، كَانَ (رَسُولُ الله ﷺ) أَجْوَدَ بِالْخَيْرِ مِنَ الرِّيحِ الْـمُرْسَلَةِ.

---

[16] Narrated by Muslim in *al-Ṣaḥīḥ*, 2:771 §1096.
[17] Narrated by al-Nasāʾī in *al-Sunan*, 4:158 §2208–2210.

> 'When Jibrīl used to visit, the Prophet ﷺ became more generous than the blowing winds.'[18]

Jibrīl's arrival would always be a message of Allah's love and affection. Since these visits used to increase in Ramaḍān far more than ordinary days, the Prophet ﷺ would also increase his charitable spending to celebrate this advent of spiritual quickening. Imam al-Nawawī deduces a number of points from this hadith, some of which we mention here.

1. The generosity of the Prophet ﷺ
2. The desirability of great acts of charity during Ramaḍān
3. Increasing the acts of charity at a righteous person's visit
4. Permissibility of establishing schools for teaching the Qur'ān.[19]

Spiritual Retreat (*al-Iʿtikāf*)

The Prophet ﷺ would always perform spiritual retreat during the last ten days of Ramaḍān. Mother of the Believers, ʿĀ'isha ﵂ reports:

إِنَّ النَّبِيَّ ﷺ كَانَ يَعْتَكِفُ الْعَشْرَ الْأَوَاخِرَ مِنْ رَمَضَانَ، حَتَّى تَوَفَّاهُ اللهُ، ثُمَّ اعْتَكَفَ أَزْوَاجُهُ مِنْ بَعْدِهِ.

> 'The Prophet ﷺ used to perform spiritual retreat during the last ten days of Ramaḍān until he ﷺ met Allah. His wives continued to perform the spiritual retreat after him ﷺ.'[20]

---

[18] Narrated by al-Bukhārī in *al-Ṣaḥīḥ*, 2:672–673 §1803.
[19] Nawawī, *Sharh Ṣaḥīḥ Muslim*, 15:69.
[20] Narrated by al-Bukhārī in *al-Ṣaḥīḥ*, 2:713 §1922.

Abū Hurayra ﷺ reports that the Prophet ﷺ used to perform spiritual retreat during the last ten days of Ramaḍān, every year. But the last Ramaḍān before he ﷺ met his Lord, he performed it for the last twenty days.[21]

Q.5. What is the value of performing ʿ*umra* during Ramaḍān?

A: The reward of performing ʿ*umra* (minor pilgrimage) during the month of Ramaḍān is equal to that of performing Hajj. Ibn ʿAbbās ﷺ reported that the Prophet ﷺ asked an Anṣārī woman why she had not performed Hajj with him ﷺ. She said that her family had two camels to fetch water. Her husband and her son travelled to Mecca on one and performed Hajj. They left the other one for the family's needs. [So, she did not have the means to go herself.] The Prophet ﷺ responded:

> 'When Ramaḍān arrives, go and perform ʿ*umra* for ʿ*umra* in Ramaḍān is like a Hajj.'[22]

Q.6. What does the chaining of Satan during Ramaḍān mean?

A: There are two main forces which lead to the commission of sin: the increased lusts of the lower self and Satan's deceitful tricks. Satan is the eternal enemy of humans. He continues to lead humans astray from the right *Dīn*, not only by himself but also with the help of a whole army of his supporters. By the great blessings of Ramaḍān, Satan is chained during this holy month. Abū Hurayra ﷺ reports that the Prophet ﷺ said:

> 'When the first night of Ramaḍān commences, every Satan as well as arrogant and disobedient

---

[21] Narrated by al-Bukhārī in *al-Ṣaḥīḥ*, 2:719 §1939.
[22] Narrated by al-Bukhārī in *al-Ṣaḥīḥ*, 2:631 §1690.

> jinn is chained; all doors of Hell are closed and not one of them is opened; all doors of Paradise are opened and none of them is closed. A herald calls all the seekers of good to advance and all the seekers of evil to retreat. Allah ﷻ frees a great number of people from Hell. This practice continues every night.'[23]

The chaining of Satan symbolises the fact that he and his minions are no longer able to deceive and the believers are not influenced by their tempting whispers. The reason for this is that the practice of fasting controls and dominates the power of the animalistic propensities within human nature, from which emanate lust and resentment; the two qualities which encourage embarking upon sin. The act of fasting on the other hand strengthens the intellectual power, which is the source of encouragement to embark upon righteous deeds. This is why the decrease of evil deeds and increase of righteous deeds becomes so evident during Ramaḍān.

One of the signs of Satan's chaining is that many sinners shun getting engaged in sin and offer repentance to Allah. Those who would not offer prayer, recite the Qur'ān or attend the gatherings of Allah's remembrance, they also abandon the sins that they used to commit openly prior to Ramaḍān. In spite of this, we find that some people persist in sin for the reason that the Satanic whispers have penetrated to the depths of their evil lower self, which is humanity's worst enemy.

The manifestations of evil and persistent commission of sins during Ramaḍān are not proof against Satan's chaining, because Ramaḍān definitely breaks the power of

---

[23] Narrated by al-Tirmidhī in *al-Sunan*, 2:61 §682.

Satan's arrogance and transgression, dulls his weapons and extinguishes the fire he has ignited.

Q.7. What does 'the opening of Paradise's doors' and 'closing of Hell's doors' mean?

A: Abū Hurayra ⁂ narrates the words of the Prophet ⁂ which state:

> 'When Ramaḍān commences, the doors of heaven are opened, the doors of Hell are closed and devils are chained.'[24]

The opening of the doors of Paradise and closing of the doors of Hell are indeed indications that people receive special divine help to perform righteous deeds, which lead them closer to Paradise and farther away from Hell. The blessings distributed during this month are far greater than during any other month. So, the person who observes the fast is protected against committing major sins. Moreover, his minor sins are also forgiven by the virtue of Ramaḍān. As a result of which he deserves Paradise.

In his commentary on this hadith in *Ḥujja Allāh al-Bāligha* (2:88), Shāh Walī Allāh Muḥaddith Dihlawī explains:

> Opening the doors of Paradise is a blessing specific to Muslims. The disbelievers and pagans on the other hand, indulge in sinfulness more than before, for they affront the signs of Allah. As opposed to this, Muslims fast, busy themselves with spiritual austerity, add more to their acts of piety and refrain from evil in this blessed month.

---

[24] Narrated by al-Bukhārī in *al-Ṣaḥīḥ*, 3:1194 §3103.

Another point is that the angels prepare Paradise for the believers (particularly those who die during this month) in view of their good deeds, which is an honour for them from the court of Allah. For this reason we can understand that the doors of Paradise are opened for them and the doors of Hell are closed for them.

Q.8. WITH WHAT FAVOURS DOES ALLAH ﷻ HONOUR THE *UMMA* OF MUHAMMAD ﷺ DURING RAMAḌĀN?

A: Jābir b. ʿAbd Allāh ؓ reports that the Prophet ﷺ said: 'My *Umma* has been favoured with five gifts in Ramaḍān which no other Prophet was given.

أَمَّا وَاحِدَةٌ: فَإِنَّهُ إِذَا كَانَ أَوَّلُ لَيْلَةٍ مِنْ شَهْرِ رَمَضَانَ، نَظَرَ اللهُ تَعَالَى إِلَيْهِمْ، وَمَنْ نَظَرَ اللهُ إِلَيْهِ لَمْ يُعَذِّبْهُ أَبَدًا.

Firstly, during its first night, Allah attends them with compassion. Whoever Allah attends with the sight of favour, He ﷻ will never torment him.

وَأَمَّا الثَّانِيَةُ: فَإِنَّ خُلُوْفَ فَمِ الصَّائِمِ أَطْيَبُ عِنْدَ اللهِ مِنْ رِيْحِ الْمِسْكِ.

Secondly, Allah ﷻ values the odour from the mouth of a fasting person towards the end of the day, more than the fragrance of musk.

وَأَمَّا الثَّالِثَةُ: فَإِنَّ الْمَلَائِكَةَ تَسْتَغْفِرُ لَهُمْ فِي كُلِّ يَوْمٍ وَلَيْلَةٍ.

Thirdly, angels seek Allah's forgiveness for them day and night.

وَأَمَّا الرَّابِعَةُ : فَإِنَّ اللهَ ﷻ يَأْمُرُ جَنَّتَهُ، فَيَقُولُ لَـهَا: اِسْتَعِدِّي وتَزَيَّنِي لِعِبَادِي. أَوْ شَكُوا أَنْ يَسْتَرِيحُوا مِنْ تَعَبِ الدُّنْيَا إِلَى دَارِي وَكَرَامَتِي.

Fourthly, Allah ﷻ commands His Paradise to be ready and ornamented for His servants. They may want to take rest in His abode of comfort and honour after the fatigue of the world. [Some of them may pass away during Ramaḍān.]

وَأَمَّا الْخَامِسَةُ: فَإِنَّهُ إِذَا كَانَ آخِرَ لَيْلَةٍ غُفِرَ لَـهُمْ.

Lastly, during the last night of Ramaḍān, they are all forgiven.'

A person from amongst the attendants asked if it was meant to be the Night of Destiny. The Prophet ﷺ replied:

لَا، أَلَمْ تَرَ إِلَى الْعُـمَّالِ يَعْمَلُوْنَ، فَإِذَا فَرَغُوْا مِنْ أَعْمَالِهِمْ وُفُّوا أُجُورَهُمْ؟

'No. Do you not see the workers are paid for their work, when they have finished it?'[25]

Q.9. What message does Ramaḍān bring to the Muslim *Umma*?

A: The message is that we must become visible embodiments of mercy and compassion for one another wherever we are and that we must start feeling the needs of others as we feel our own. It is really sad that there are affluent people amongst the Muslims who spend the day of their fast inside air conditioned buildings and vehicles

[25] Narrated by al- in *Shu'ab al-Īmān*, 3:303 §3603; and al-Mundhirī in *al-Targhīb wa al-Tarhīb*, 2:56 §1477.

and sit at dinner tables decorated with various types of food and drink at the fast-breaking time, but have not the slightest of feeling for their poor and impoverished Muslim brothers out on the streets and roads. We may possibly have somebody in our neighbourhood who started his fast at dawn with a few swallows of water and must look to others to provide something to eat at dusk. Ramaḍān brings us the message that we must look after the penniless and hungry Muslim brothers, who cannot afford to buy food and dress for themselves or their children. At the same time, it also educates us to refrain from social and spiritual ailments such as backbiting, slandering, deceit, jealousy, lying, pretence, malice, quibbling and fault-finding.

Q.10. What are the merits of night vigil of Ramaḍān?

A: Night vigil here means to worship, particularly in the form of offering prayer (i.e., *qiyām al-layl*). Its importance in Ramaḍān is vital. The Holy Prophet ﷺ had a routine of busying himself with prayer, glorifying Allah ﷻ, invoking His unity and reciting the Qur'ān at length. Abū Hurayra ؓ reports:

كَانَ رَسُوْلُ اللهِ ﷺ يُرَغِّبُ فِي قِيَامِ رَمَضَانَ مِنْ غَيْرِ أَنْ يَأْمُرَهُمْ بِعَزِيْمَةٍ، وَيَقُوْلُ: مَنْ قَامَ رَمَضَانَ إِيْمَانًا وَاحْتِسَابًا ، غُفِرَ لَهُ مَا تَقَدَّمَ مِنْ ذَنْبِهِ.

> 'Allah's Messenger ﷺ used to encourage his Companions ؓ to stand in Ramaḍān without obligating it upon them. He would say: 'Whoever stands at night in Ramaḍān with faith and hope

> for reward, all his previous sins will be forgiven."[26]

This hadith clearly states the significance of night vigil of Ramaḍān. The *tarāwīḥ* prayer is its significant form, which is formally called *qiyām al-layl* (night vigil). The amount of prayer performed during this month because of *tarāwīḥ* is more than during any other month of the year. The purpose is to encourage Allah's servants to spend the greatest amount of time possible during Ramaḍān nights in worship, remembrance and contemplation and so equip themselves with divine pleasure. This is why Ramaḍān nights require keeping a vigil. The traditions mention that Allah ﷻ brings His special favours down to the lowest heaven, closest to his servants. Then He calls them as it suits Him:

> Is there anyone to ask so that I grant him his wish? Is there anyone to repent so that I accept his repentance? Is there anyone to seek forgiveness so that I may forgive him?[27]

Allah's mercy invites everyone to come under the protection of divine forgiveness and benevolence during Ramaḍān nights. The sad thing is that human beings sacrifice such precious moments of success with seeking mercy and forgiveness, for the deep sleep of utter negligence. Unfortunate people fail to receive their share of Allah's mercy by drawing the sheet of sleep over themselves, while the calls of the Lord's mercy keep shaking his dead soul. As Iqbāl presents it:

ہم تو مائل بہ کرم ہیں کوئی سائل ہی نہیں
راہ دکھلائیں کسے راہرو منزل ہی نہیں

---

[26] Narrated by al-Tirmidhī in *al-Sunan*, 2:161 §808.
[27] Narrated by al-Bayhaqī in *Shu'ab al-Īmān*, 3:335 §3695.

> Alas! There is not a single seeker, although we do incline to grant. Who should we guide where there is not a single traveller?'

Q.11. What is the significance of reciting the Qurʾān during Ramaḍān?

A: The Qurʾān is a unique book, in the sense that reciting a single letter from it would earn you ten righteous deeds. ʿAbd Allah b. Masʿūd ﵁ narrates a Prophetic tradition as follows:

مَنْ قَرَأَ حَرْفاً مِنْ كِتَابِ اللهِ فَلَهُ بِهِ حَسَنَةٌ ، وَالْحَسَنَةُ بِعَشْرِ أَمْثَالِهَا، لَا أَقُوْلُ: الم حَرْفٌ ؛ وَلَكِنْ أَلِفٌ حَرْفٌ ، وَلَامٌ حَرْفٌ ، وَمِيْمٌ حَرْفٌ.

> 'Whoever recites a letter from the book of Allah will earn one righteous deed and one righteous deed comes with ten like it. I do not say that *alif*, *lām*, *mīm* is one letter but *alif* is a letter, *lām* is another letter and *mīm* is another one.'[28]

The recitation of the Qurʾān is one of the most prominent acts of worship. Nuʿmān b. Bashīr ﵁ says that the Prophet ﷺ said:

أَفْضَلُ عِبَادَةِ أُمَّتِي قِرَاءَةُ الْقُرْآنِ.

> 'The most prominent worship for my *Umma* is the recitation of the Qurʾān.'[29]

This remarkable book with all its pre-eminence, was revealed in the month of Ramaḍān. This shows the strength of connection between the two. So, the person

---

[28] Narrated by al-Tirmidhī in *al-Sunan*, 5:33 §2910.

[29] Narrated by al-Bayhaqī in *Shuʿab al-Īmān*, 2:354 §2022.

reciting the Qurʾān indeed deems to solidify that connection firmly.

A number of Prophetic traditions prove that the Prophet ﷺ would always recite the Qurʾān at length during Ramaḍān. He would also recite it by heart to Jibrīl ؑ. ʿAbd Allāh b. ʿAbbās ؓ narrates:

كَانَ يَلْقَاهُ فِي كُلِّ لَيْلَةٍ مِنْ رَمَضَانَ، فَيُدَارِسُهُ الْقُرْآنَ.

> 'Jibrīl used to visit the Prophet ﷺ every night during Ramaḍān and they would recite the Qurʾān to each other.'[30]

Moreover, the Qurʾān will intercede on behalf of those who recite it regularly. ʿAbd Allah b. ʿAmr ؓ reported that the Prophet ﷺ said:

> 'Both of the Qurʾān and 'Fast' will intercede on behalf of Allah's servants. 'Fast' will say: 'O my Lord! This person would resist his lust for food and lowly (voluptuous) desires all day long. So, please accept my intercession on his behalf (and forgive him).' The Qurʾān will say: 'It was I who kept him with vigil at night. So, please accept my intercession on his behalf (and forgive him).' Then the Prophet ﷺ said: 'The intercession of both will be accepted.''[31]

Q.12. What is the importance of eating pre-dawn meal for fasting?

A: Hadiths mention the importance and blessings of eating the *suḥūr*[32] a great deal. Our holy Prophet ﷺ

---

[30] Narrated by al-Bukhārī in *al-Ṣaḥīḥ*, 1:7 §6.

[31] Narrated by Aḥmad b. Ḥanbal in *al-Musnad*, 2:174 §6626.

[32] This means morning. It refers to the food Muslims take before the break of dawn to keep their fast during the day.

would regularly start his fast with something to eat, as a pre-dawn meal for fasting and would also tell others to do so. You can find the matter made clear in some of the traditions mentioned below.

Anas 🅐 narrates that the Prophet 🅐 said:

$$\text{تَسَحَّرُوا، فَإِنَّ فِي السُّحُورِ بَرَكَةً.}$$

'Eat pre-dawn meal for fasting, for it contains blessings.'[33]

Abū Saʿīd al-Khudrī 🅐 narrates that the Prophet 🅐 said:

$$\text{اَلسُّحُورُ أَكْلُهُ بَرَكَةٌ، فَلَا تَدَعُوهُ.}$$

'Eating pre-dawn meal for fasting is a blessing. So, do not miss it.'[34]

He also narrates the hadith:

$$\text{فَإِنَّ اللهَ وَمَلَائِكَتَهُ يُصَلُّونَ عَلَى الْمُتَسَحِّرِينَ.}$$

'Allah and His angels shower mercy upon those who eat pre-dawn meal for fasting.'[35]

ʿAmr b. al-ʿĀs 🅐 narrates that the Prophet 🅐 said:

$$\text{فَضْلُ مَا بَيْنَ صِيَامِنَا وَصِيَامِ أَهْلِ الْكِتَابِ أَكْلَةُ السَّحَرِ.}$$

'The difference between our fast and that of the People of the Book is that of eating pre-dawn meal for fasting.'[36]

ʿIrbāḍ b. Sāriya 🅐 says that he heard the Prophet 🅐 say, as he advised people to eat pre-dawn meal for fasting:

---

[33] Narrated by Muslim in *al-Ṣaḥīḥ*, 2:770 §1095.

[34] Narrated by Aḥmad b. Ḥanbal in *al-Musnad*, 3:12 §11102.

[35] Ibid.

[36] Narrated by Muslim in *al-Ṣaḥīḥ*, 2:770 §1096.

هَلُمُّوا إِلَى الْغَدَاءِ الْـمُـبَارَكِ.

'Come to the blessed dinner!'[37]

Pre-dawn meal for fasting (*al-suḥūr*) undoubtedly holds an important place in fasting. Apart from its spiritual blessings, it helps us keep the fast during the day. It also strengthens our inclination towards fasting. Adding to this, it also has a connection with night vigil, for this is the time of Allah's remembrance, offering prayers and supplications. Another distinction of this time is that it is a time when divine mercy descends and allows for the acceptance of supplications and a positive response to sought-for forgiveness.

Q.13. What is the importance of fast breaking in Ramaḍān?

A: During Ramaḍān, it is also important to mark the end of the fast with *al-ifṭār*[38]. Sahl b. Saʿd ﷺ narrates that the Prophet ﷺ said:

لَا يَزَالُ النَّاسُ بِخَيْرٍ مَا عَجَّلُوا الْفِطْرَ.

'The people (of my *Umma*) will remain in good state as long as they hasten fast breaking.'[39]

Abū Hurayra ﷺ narrates a hadith in which the Prophet ﷺ narrates that Allah ﷻ said:

أَحَبُّ عِبَادِي إِلَيَّ أَعْجَلُهُمْ فِطْرًا.

[37] Narrated by Muslim in *al-Ṣaḥīḥ*, 2:770 §1095.
[38] This word in Arabic means to eat, drink or do something that marks the breaking of the fast: the breaking of the fast, if done during the day, and its completion if done after dusk.
[39] Narrated by Muslim in *al-Ṣaḥīḥ*, 2:771 §1098.

'I love those amongst my servants who hasten *al-iftār* the most.'[40]

Ya'la b. Murra 🕮 reported the Prophet 🕮 to have said that Allah 🕮 likes three things:

1. To delay pre-dawn meal for fasting to the last time (before the break of dawn)

2. To hasten fast breaking (after dusk)

3. To place one hand on the other while standing in prayer.[41]

This shows the importance not only of the fast breaking itself, but also that of hastening it. Amongst other numerous spiritual blessings evidently attached to the time of fast breaking, we find 'Abd Allah b. 'Amr b. al-'Ās 🕮 who reported the Prophet 🕮 as saying:

'The supplication made at the time of fast breaking by the one who has fasted that day, is not rejected.'

---

[40] Narrated by Ibn Ḥibbān in *al-Ṣaḥīḥ*, 4:588 §1670.
[41] Narrated by Ibn Mājah in *al-Sunan*, 2:364 §1753.

2. Rulings of Shariah regarding Ramaḍān

Q.14. What does the رُؤْيَةُ الْهِلاَل (moon sighting) stand for?

A: It is an Arabic word which means to see, to have sight of something, to view, etc. In this context, it means to sight the crescent at the start of each lunar month, so as to be able to count the dates and months correctly and keep the calendar accurate. In this way, it also helps us to specify important days and nights which we are meant to celebrate, such as the days of *ʿĪd*, the month of Ramaḍān, the fifteenth night of Shaʿbān, etc.

Q.15. What are the decisive factors of moon sighting?

A: Usually there are four important factors:

1. The brightness of the horizon; its being unclouded
2. The cleanness of the air; its being unpolluted
3. The sharpness of the eye
4. Good weather conditions

Q.16. What prayer should we say when we see the crescent?

A: ʿAbd Allāh b. ʿUmar ﵁ says that the Prophet ﷺ used to say the following prayer after sighting the moon:

اَللَّهُمَّ أَهِلَّهُ عَلَيْنَا بِالأَمْنِ وَالْإِيْمَانِ وَالسَّلَامَةِ وَالسَّلامِ وَالتَّوْفِيْقِ لِمَا تُحِبُّ وَتَرْضَى. رَبُّنَا وَرَبُّكَ اللهُ.

> 'O Allah! Let the moon rise to us with security, faith, peace, Islam and your assistance to commit what you love and please. O Moon! Our and your Lord is Allah.'[42]

Q.17. Are we allowed to fast on the 30th of Shaʿbān if the the moon is not visible on the 29th?

A: Some people keep fast on particular days, such as fasting on Mondays. If the 30th of Shaʿbān falls on one such day, for example on a Monday for the person who keeps fast on Mondays, he can keep an optional fast that day. Otherwise, we have been advised not to keep fast. Abū Hurayra ﵁ narrates that the Prophet ﷺ said:

> 'Do not keep fast one or two days before Ramaḍān (commences) except for the person whose routine of keeping fast falls on that day.'[43]

---

[42] Narrated by al-Haythamī in *Mawārid al-Ẓamʾān*, 1:589 §2374.

[43] Narrated by Muslim in *al-Ṣaḥīḥ*, 2:762 §1082.

Q.18. People are supposed to start Ramaḍān by the sighting of the moon. The validity of the sighting depends upon the witness borne by the claimants of the sighting. If the horizon is clear, what is the minimum number of witnesses required for a sighting to be valid?

A: If the person who claims to have made the sighting, has not come from a place higher than the town or locality where other people were not able to sight the moon, despite all their efforts and a clear horizon, his claim will not be accepted. In this case, the number of people who sight the moon must be big enough to assure the proof of the sighting. In the case of ʿīd, however, two reliable righteous Muslims would be enough to prove the moon sighting.

Q.19. How many people are required to bear witness in order to prove a moon sighting if the horizon is cloudy?

A: If the horizon is cloudy or covered with dust or something else that prevents easy and reliable moon sighting, one righteous person's witness to have sighted the moon would be enough. The same is true in the case of a person who is apparently religious and his transgression unknown. Abū Dāwūd reports that ʿIkrima ؓ said:

> 'In one instance people fell in doubt about the sighting of the moon. They made up their minds that they would not pray tarāwīḥ that night. Nor would they keep fast the following day. At that time, a Bedouin came from Ḥarra (a relatively high place), who told them he had sighted the

> moon. They took him to the Prophet ﷺ. The Prophet ﷺ asked him if he bore witness that Allah has no partners and Muhammad is His Messenger. He bore witness to that and to have sighted the moon. The Prophet ﷺ instructed Bilāl to make the announcement to pray *tarāwīḥ* that night and keep fast the following day. So he did.'[44]

Q.20. What does *al-tarāwīḥ* mean and how are they performed?

A: The word *al-tarāwīḥ* is the plural of *al-tarwīḥa*, which means 'to take a period of rest'. So, *tarāwīḥ* would mean 'to take many periods of rest'. The prescribed number of cycles is 20. It is meritorious to take a short break for rest after every four (which means four breaks altogether). Such was the practice of the Companions ﷺ. This is the reason it has been called *tarāwīḥ*. It is an emphasised Prophetic practice, which is a strongly recommended act for every Muslim man and woman. One is not allowed to miss it.

The *qiyām* of Ramaḍān (offering abundant prayer) has been valued highly. Abū Hurayra ﷺ reported that the Prophet ﷺ used to awaken the desire for the *qiyām* of Ramaḍān strongly and encouraged people to realise the *qiyām* of Ramaḍān. He ﷺ would often say:

> 'Whoever performs the *qiyām* of Ramaḍān with faith and intention of receiving its reward, will have his previous sins forgiven.'[45]

The time of *tarāwīḥ* prayer is after *ʿIshāʾ* prayer and before *al-witr* prayer. It is more meritorious to perform it

---

[44] Narrated by Abū Dawūd in *al-Sunan*, 2:289 §2341.

[45] Narrated by Muslim in *al-Ṣaḥīḥ*, 1:523 §759.

towards the last part of the night. In our own times however, to bring it back in the early part of the night would take precedence because it eases the matter for people.

Q.21. What is the number of cycles in *Tarāwīḥ* prayer?

A: The authentic opinion confirms that the number of cycles of *tarāwīḥ* is 20. That is the juristic opinion held by all four schools of law amongst Ahl al-Sunna, which make up the overwhelming majority of the Muslim *Umma*.

Mother of the Believers, ʿĀʾisha ﷺ reports that the Prophet ﷺ prayed an optional prayer in his mosque during one Ramaḍān night. The Companions joined him in that prayer. The next night he ﷺ did the same and a bigger gathering joined him. A bigger number gathered the third or the fourth night but the Prophet ﷺ did not attend them. Then the following morning he told them the only cautious thought that prevented his arrival the previous night, was his concern that it could obligate that particular prayer upon them. This incident occurred in Ramaḍān (it was *tarāwīḥ* prayer).[46]

The narration of Ibn Khuzayma and Ibn Ḥibbān reads as follows:

> The Prophet ﷺ used to encourage them to perform the *qiyām* of Ramaḍān without a strict imperative. He would often say, 'Whoever performs the *qiyām* of Ramaḍān with true faith and hope for its reward will have all his previous sins forgiven.' The Prophet ﷺ continued to perform the *qiyām* of Ramaḍān as mentioned (individually without congregation). This

---

[46] Narrated by al-Bukhārī in *al-Ṣaḥīḥ*, 1:380 §1077 & 2:708 §1908; Muslim in *al-Ṣaḥīḥ*, 1:524 §761; al-Nasāʾī in *al-Sunan*, 2:337 §1604; and Abū Dawūd in *al-Sunan*, 1:49 §1373.

continued through the time of Abū Bakr's Caliphate and the early years of ʿUmar's Caliphate 🙠. Until ʿUmar 🙠 appointed Ubayy b. Kaʿb 🙠 to lead them and collected them to follow him in *tarāwīḥ*. This was the first time when Muslims formally followed one Imam to offer their *Tarāwīḥ* prayer.[47]

Ibn Hajar al-ʿAsqalānī states in his book *Talkhīṣ al-Ḥabīr* (2:21) that the Prophet 🙠 led the Companions 🙠 a twenty cycles *tarāwīḥ* prayer for two nights. When people gathered the third night, he did not come out of his chamber. He 🙠 then told them the following morning, 'I was worried lest it be an obligation upon you, then you won't be able to fulfil it.'

ʿAbd Allāh b. ʿAbbās 🙠 reports that the Prophet 🙠 used to offer twenty cycles of *tarāwīḥ* apart from *al-witr* prayer during Ramaḍān.[48]

Sāʾib b. Yazīd 🙠 reported that they used to offer twenty cycles of *tarāwīḥ* during ʿUmar's Caliphate.[49]

This narration explicitly states that the total cycles of *tarāwīḥ* prayer are 20. Such is the consensus of all four schools of thought of Ahl al-Sunna. Such has been the practice of the two sacred cities of Mecca and Medina till today. They offer twenty cycles of *tarāwīḥ* and you can watch it live on TV.

---

[47] Narrated by Ibn Khuzayma in *al-Ṣaḥīḥ*, 3:388 §2207; and Ibn Ḥibbān in *al-Ṣaḥīḥ*, 1:353 §141.

[48] Narrated by al-Ṭabarānī in *al-Muʿjam al-Kabīr*, 11:311 §12102; al-Ṭabarānī in *al-Muʿjam al-Awsaṭ*, 1:243 §798 & 5:324 §5440; and Ibn Abī Shayba in *al-Muṣannaf*, 2:164 §7692.

[49] Narrated by al-Bayhaqī in *al-Sunan al-Kubrā*, 2:699 §4617.

Q.22. What is the prescribed amount of Qur'ān recitations during *Tarāwīḥ*? Do we have to recite all of the Qur'ān once during Ramaḍān?

A: It is Sunna to recite the whole of the Qur'ān in *Tarāwīḥ*, once in Ramaḍān, provided that the followers are not utterly dejected and weary. It is important to consider the conditions of the followers and their circumstances while reciting the Qur'ān in *tarāwīḥ*. Nor should the recitation be too fast, so as to prevent the occurrence of disturbance and disorder.

Q.23. What is the correct method of reciting the whole of the Qur'ān in one night during Ramaḍān?

A: The *shabīna*[50] is quite prevalent in our times and is on the increase. It is indeed against the Prophetic practice, for the Prophet ﷺ used to advise his Companions ؓ to content themselves with the recitation of the whole of the Qur'ān once a month. ʿAbd Allāh b. ʿAmr ؓ used to recite the whole of the Qur'ān once every day. The Prophet ﷺ summoned him and instructed him to recite the Qur'ān once a month. He said he was able to do more. The Prophet ﷺ allowed him to reduce the time span to twenty days, then to ten days and finally to seven days, but did not allow anything lesser than that. The words of the Prophet ﷺ read:

فَاقْرَأْهُ فِي كُلِّ سَبْعٍ.

---

[50] It comes from the Persian word *shab* which means night. It is the custom of reciting the whole of the Qur'ān in optional prayer during one or two or three nights of the last ten nights of Ramaḍān.

> 'You can finish the whole of the Qur'ān in seven days (for the minimum).'[51]

This hadith clarifies that the custom of reciting the whole of the Qur'ān in a single night is against the Sunna. However, we are allowed to do it in 3 nights during the last seven or ten nights of Ramaḍān. We must also keep a few points in our minds, that the recitation must be slow enough for listeners to understand the words being recited, along with the meanings if they know enough Arabic. One is not allowed to recite too fast. The length of the recitation should not be such as to exhaust minds. As soon as people start feeling dull, the recitation should stop.

Jundub b. ʿAbd Allāh al-Bajalī reports that the Prophet ﷺ said:

> 'Recite the Qur'ān for as long as your heart follows your tongue and leave it when they differ.'[52]

The use of loudspeakers for this purpose in Islamic countries is unsuitable because listening to the recitation of the Qur'ān is obligatory. The non-attendant would be rendered sinful. So, it is the best and most reasonable position not to use them at all. In cases when they are necessary, they must be confined to the internal sound system, so that the sound does not reach the streets.

Q.24. Can a woman lead other women in *tarāwīḥ* prayer?

A: It is a matter of difference amongst jurists whether only women can have their own congregational prayer (in the case of non-obligatory prayers such as *tarāwīḥ*). Some

---

[51] Narrated by Muslim in *al-Ṣaḥīḥ*, 2:813 §1159.

[52] Narrated by Muslim in *al-Ṣaḥīḥ*, 4:2054 §2667.

jurists have held that the Shariah dislikes it. Imam al-Marghīnānī a prominent Hanafite jurist, says in his outstanding treatise, namely *al-Hidāya* (1:84):

وَيُكْرَهُ لِلنِّسَاءِ أَنْ يُّصَلِّيْنَ وَحْدَهُنَّ الْجَمَاعَةَ ... فَإِنْ فَعَلْنَ قَامَتِ الْإِمَامَةُ وَسَطَهُنَّ.

> A women-only congregational prayer is disliked. ... If it is done, their Imam will stand in the middle of the front row.

However, traditions do mention that Mother of the Believers, ʿĀʾisha ﵦ used to lead women-only congregational prayer. Al-Ḥākim has mentioned a tradition about her that she used to stand in the middle of the row while leading women's prayer.[53]

This tradition proves the permissibility of women-only congregational prayer, if the purpose is to give them religious education and to promote an inclination towards acts of worship. The Imam will stand in the middle of the front row. In the case of the *ʿīd* prayer, she can also deliver an oration. The jurists have clarified that a woman can lead other women in prayer and a pre-pubescent can be Imam of other pre-pubescents.

---

[53] Narrated by Al-Ḥākim in *al-Mustadrak*, 1:320 §731.

3. The Fast

Q.25. What is the literal and legal meaning of fasting?

A: The Arabic word for fasting is *al-ṣawm*. Literally, it means to desist from eating, drinking and marital coitus from dawn to dusk. The Qur'ān states:

(وَكُلُواْ وَٱشْرَبُواْ حَتَّىٰ يَتَبَيَّنَ لَكُمُ ٱلْخَيْطُ ٱلْأَبْيَضُ مِنَ ٱلْخَيْطِ ٱلْأَسْوَدِ مِنَ ٱلْفَجْرِ ثُمَّ أَتِمُّواْ ٱلصِّيَامَ إِلَى ٱلَّيْلِ)

Eat and drink until the white thread of dawn becomes distinct to you (separated) from the black thread (of night). Then complete the fast till dusk.[54]

The white thread means 'the break of dawn (when daylight breaks horizontally)' and the black thread means the darkness prior to it (when a light appears vertically for a short time and then disappears).

Q.26. What is the value and legal status of *al-ṣawm* in the light of the Qur'ān and hadith?

A: In this regard, Allah ﷻ states in the Qur'ān:

(يَـٰٓأَيُّهَا ٱلَّذِينَ ءَامَنُواْ كُتِبَ عَلَيۡكُمُ ٱلصِّيَامُ كَمَا كُتِبَ عَلَى ٱلَّذِينَ مِن قَبۡلِكُمۡ لَعَلَّكُمۡ تَتَّقُونَ)

[54] Qur'ān, *al-Baqara*, 2:187.

O Believers! Fasting is prescribed for you as it was prescribed for the people before you so that you may become pious.[55]

Abū Hurayra ﷺ reports that the Prophet ﷺ said:

مَنْ صَامَ رَمَضَانَ إِيْمَانًا وَاحْتِسَابًا غُفِرَ لَهُ مَا تَقَدَّمَ مِنْ ذَنْبِهِ.

'Whoever keeps the fast of Ramaḍān with faith and hope for (pure intention of) its reward, will have all his previous sins forgiven.'[56]

The Prophet ﷺ said:

اَلصَّوْمُ جُنَّةٌ مِنَ النَّارِ كَجُنَّةِ أَحَدِكُمْ مِنَ الْقِتَالِ.

'Fasting is a shield against the Fire of Hell, just like one of yours' (against a fighting enemy) in the middle of a battle.'[57]

Abū Hurayra ﷺ reports that the Prophet ﷺ said:

كُلُّ عَمَلِ ابْنِ آدَمَ يُضَاعَفُ ، اَلْحَسَنَةُ بِعَشْرِ أَمْثَالِهَا إِلَى سَبْعِمِائَةِ ضِعْفٍ إِلَى مَا شَاءَ اللهُ. يَقُوْلُ اللهُ تَعَالَى: إِلَّا الصَّوْمَ فَإِنَّهُ لِي، وَأَنَا أَجْزِي بِهِ.

'The strength of each human deed's reward is increased from ten times to seven hundred times, to as many times as Allah ﷻ wills per righteous deed; except for the act of fasting. Allah ﷻ declares: It is only for Me and only I shall award its recompense.'[58]

---

[55] Qur'ān, *al-Baqara*, 2:183.
[56] Narrated by al-Bukhārī in *al-Ṣaḥīḥ*, 1:22 §38.
[57] Narrated by al-Nasā'ī in *al-Sunan*, 2:637 §2230–2231.
[58] Narrated by Ibn Mājah in *al-Sunan*, 2:305 §1638.

These hadiths explain that based on the purity and sincerity behind it, one righteous deed can be rewarded for as many as seven hundred deeds or even more; as many as Allah ﷻ wills. But the case of fasting is different. It is beyond limit, estimation and measurement. Only Allah ﷻ knows the exact amount.

Below we mention some of the reasons for such value.

1. Fasting is hidden from people. Only Allah ﷻ knows you are fasting. Other acts of worship are not like this. People can see you perform them. So, fasting is only for Allah ﷻ and this is the meaning of saying 'it is only for Me'.

2. Fasting is an act that involves manifest temperance, hardship, self-denial, hunger pangs and dehydration. It trains you in forbearance, self-restraint and conquering the desires of the lower self. It is like a goldsmith's furnace that burns the pollutants away.

3. It does not involve display, whereas other acts of worship are apparent, such as prayer, pilgrimage and many others, and can pollute the intention by a pretentious instinct.

4. Being beyond the need for food or drink is one of Allah's attributes. Although a human being can never resemble Allah ﷻ, this practice, a '*kind of moulding oneself in the frame of one of His attributes*', can bring the enormous blessing of Allah's proximity.

5. Allah ﷻ has disclosed to His creation the reward of each deed except fasting. He ﷻ has kept it to Himself.

6. Fasting is an act of worship which is not visible to anyone except to Allah ﷻ.

7. Allah ﷻ has connected it to Himself to show its honour, loftiness and significance. It is like describing the

kaba as the 'House of Allah' to show its high rank. Otherwise, every place and house belongs to Allah ﷻ.

8. A fasting person absorbs angelic qualities through this act. Allah ﷻ loves him for this reason.

9. The reward of patience and forbearance knows no limits. This is why Allah ﷻ has attributed the reward of fasting to Himself, stating 'I am its reward'.

Q.27. Which pillar amongst the pillars of Islam is fasting?

A: It is the third pillar of Islam. It falls after the witness of monotheism (*al-tawhīd*) and messengership (*al-risāla*) and prayer. In a hadith mentioned earlier, Abū Hurayra ؓ has reported that the Prophet ﷺ said,

> 'Whoever keeps the fasts of Ramaḍān with faith and hope for (pure intention of) its reward will have all his previous sins forgiven.'[59]

Q.28. What type of worship is fasting?

A: It is a physical act of worship, which is the best means to self-purification. Abū Hurayra ؓ reports that the Prophet ﷺ said:

> لِكُلِّ شَيْءٍ زَكَاةٌ وَزَكَاةُ الْجَسَدِ الصَّوْمُ.

> 'Everything has a purifier and the purifier of the body is fasting.'[60]

Fasting is secret, private and silent as well as free of ostentation and the display of an act of worship. The Prophet ﷺ said of the fast-keeper:

---

[59] Narrated by al-Bukhārī in *al-Ṣaḥīḥ*, 2:709 §1910.

[60] Narrated by Ibn Mājah in *al-Sunan*, 2:361 §1745.

مَنْ صَامَ يَوْمًا فِي سَبِيْلِ اللهِ ، بَعَّدَ اللهُ وَجْهَهُ عَنِ النَّارِ سَبْعِيْنَ خَرِيْفًا.

'Whoever keeps fast for one day in the cause of Allah is taken away from the Fire to a distance of seventy years.'[61]

Q.29. When was fasting obligated?

A: It was obligated in the second year of hegira, about a fortnight after the redirection of the *qibla*[62] towards *kaʿba*. The verse of the Qurʾān that obligated the fasting of Ramaḍān, was revealed in the month of Shaʿbān. It states:

(شَهْرُ رَمَضَانَ ٱلَّذِىٓ أُنزِلَ فِيهِ ٱلْقُرْءَانُ هُدًى لِّلنَّاسِ وَبَيِّنَـٰتٍ مِّنَ ٱلْهُدَىٰ وَٱلْفُرْقَانِ ۚ فَمَن شَهِدَ مِنكُمُ ٱلشَّهْرَ فَلْيَصُمْهُ)

The month of Ramaḍān (is that) in which the Qurʾān has been sent down as guidance for mankind, containing clear Signs which lead (to the straight road) and distinguish (the Truth from falsehood). Therefore, he who witnesses this month must fast in it.[63]

Islamic injunctions came gradually. The injunction of monotheism (*al-tawhīd*), prophethood (*al-risāla*), prayer and others prior to hegira were already in place and gradually became part of a Muslim's life. That is why the obligation of fasting was delayed and came after the others were firm. Before the obligation of fasting the

[61] Narrated by al-Bukhārī in *al-Ṣaḥīḥ*, 3:1044 §2685.

[62] The direction of the *kaʿba*, in Mecca, toward which Muslims face when praying.

[63] Qurʾān, *al-Baqara*, 2:185.

Prophet ﷺ used to fast on the tenth of Muḥarram, a practice cancelled by its obligation. Ibn ʿUmar ﵄ reported:

> 'The holy Prophet ﷺ fasted on the tenth of Muḥarram and directed us to do so. It was cancelled after the obligation of the fasting of Ramaḍān.'[64]

Q.30. Who is fasting obligated upon?

A: Islam has obligated the fasting of Ramaḍān upon every mature Muslim of sound mind, man and woman across the world. Allah ﷻ states:

(شَهْرُ رَمَضَانَ ٱلَّذِىٓ أُنزِلَ فِيهِ ٱلْقُرْءَانُ هُدًى لِّلنَّاسِ وَبَيِّنَٰتٍ مِّنَ ٱلْهُدَىٰ وَٱلْفُرْقَانِ ۚ فَمَن شَهِدَ مِنكُمُ ٱلشَّهْرَ فَلْيَصُمْهُ)

The month of Ramaḍān (is that) in which the Qurʾān has been sent down as guidance for mankind, containing clear Signs which lead (to the straight road) and distinguish (the Truth from falsehood). Therefore, he who witnesses this month must fast in it.[65]

Non-performance of an obligation is a punishable offence. Since Islam is an easy *Dīn* to practice, it does not believe in coercion. The Qurʾān states:

(لَآ إِكْرَاهَ فِى ٱلدِّينِ)

There is no compulsion in Dīn *(Religion).*[66]

Some concession has been made for travel, illness, pregnancy and similar difficult circumstances. In case of any of these occurrences during Ramaḍān, the affected

---

[64] Narrated by al-Bukhārī in *al-Ṣaḥīḥ*, 2:669 §1793.

[65] Qurʾān, *al-Baqara*, 2:185.

[66] Qurʾān, *al-Baqara*, 2:256.

person is allowed to postpone the fast. One has to fast for the days he has missed when he is able.

Q.31. Was fasting obligated upon the communities prior to us?

A: Yes, it was. This is clear from the following verse:

(يَـٰٓأَيُّهَا ٱلَّذِينَ ءَامَنُوا۟ كُتِبَ عَلَيۡكُمُ ٱلصِّيَامُ كَمَا كُتِبَ عَلَى ٱلَّذِينَ مِن قَبۡلِكُمۡ لَعَلَّكُمۡ تَتَّقُونَ.)

> *O Believers! Fasting is prescribed for you as it was prescribed for the people before you, so that you may become pious.*[67]

A careful study of hadith literature, history, the Torah and the Bible reveals that fasting was known and practiced by pre-Islamic communities. We mention here some of them.

1. The Quraysh of Mecca used to fast on the tenth of Muḥarram, for this was the day they would offer coverings for the *kaʿba*.[68]

2. The Jews of Medina used to fast on the tenth of Muḥarram, for this was the day the Israelites were liberated from the Pharaoh.[69]

3. The *Encyclopaedia Judaica* confirms:

> Jews and Christians used to fast to mark repentance, to expiate for sins or even lower objectives. It was simply observed as a ritual. In early times, it was observed as a sign of mourning.[70]

[67] Qurʾān, *al-Baqara*, 2:183.
[68] Narrated by al-Bukhārī in *al-Ṣaḥīḥ*, 2:578 §1515.
[69] Narrated by al-Bukhārī in *al-Ṣaḥīḥ*, 2:704 §1900.
[70] *Encyclopaedia Judaica*, Second Ed., 6:719–723.

It seems that fasting had been taken out of context and lost its original relevance. People associated it with their particular interests. It is Islam, which introduced it to humanity as a purposeful system of spiritual training, giving it a vast spectrum of influence in human life and attached highly regarded objectives to it. A check is placed upon many lawful longings and valid desires during the act of fasting. A true member of the Prophet Muhammad's *Umma* readily applies all such restrictions to himself. He bases his practice upon the basis of his faith, that it is the most useful thing for both his body and soul.

In addition, different religions place the responsibility of fasting upon different classes within their relative societies. Zoroaster's followers, for example, obligate it only upon their religious leaders; Hindus only upon the Brahman; and the Greeks only upon their women. The imbalance, likewise, has also affected the timings.

In Islam, however, it has been obligated upon every mature man and woman of sound mind during the same month of Ramaḍān.

Q.32. How many kinds of fast are there?

A: There are 8 kinds of fast.

al-farḍ al-muʿayyan (specific obligation)	*al-farḍ ghayr al-muʿayyan* (unspecified obligation)
al-wājib al-muʿayyan (specific act of worship)	*al-wājib ghayr al-muʿayyan* (unspecified act of worship)
al-masnūn (founded on the Prophetic practice)	*al-nafl* (voluntary; supererogatory)
al-makrūh (a disliked or	*al-ḥarām* (forbidden)

offensive act)

Q.33. What are *al-farḍ al-muʿayyan* and *al-farḍ ghayr al-muʿayyan* fast?

A: *Al-Farḍ al-muʿayyan* means 'specific obligation'. This covers the fasts of Ramaḍān, which has been obligated for that particular month. The Qur'ān states:

﴿يَـٰٓأَيُّهَا ٱلَّذِينَ ءَامَنُوا۟ كُتِبَ عَلَيْكُمُ ٱلصِّيَامُ كَمَا كُتِبَ عَلَى ٱلَّذِينَ مِن قَبْلِكُمْ لَعَلَّكُمْ تَتَّقُونَ﴾

O Believers! Fasting is prescribed for you as it was prescribed for the people before you, so that you may become pious.[71]

Al-Farḍ ghayr al-muʿayyan means 'unspecified obligation'. If one misses one or more fasts during Ramaḍān, he is obliged to make it up at any time during the rest of the months in his life. This is called *al-farḍ ghayr al-muʿayyan*.

Q.34. What are *al-wājib al-muʿayyan* and *al-wājib ghayr al-muʿayyan* fast?

A: If somebody has vowed to fast on a particular day, say on the first of Rajab, if he has passed his exam, it will be an imperative for him to fast on that particular day once he has passed the exam. Such a fast is called *al-wājib al-muʿayyan*. If he has vowed to fast one or two or more unspecified days if he passes his exam, he can fast whenever he wants in his lifetime once he has passed the exam. This is called *al-wājib ghayr al-muʿayyan*. So the fast is a religious expatiation.

---

[71] Qur'ān, *al-Baqara*, 2:183.

Q.35. What is meant by *al-Masnūn* fast?

A: The fast that was performed by the Prophet ﷺ other than the obligatory and imperative ones, are called *al-masnūn*. In addition, the Prophet ﷺ also encouraged his *Umma* to perform them. Here is a brief description.

The fast on ninth and tenth of *Muḥarram*

Shariah has given this fast great value. Abū Qatāda ؓ reports that the Prophet ﷺ was asked about the fast of ʿ*āshūrā*ʾ (the tenth of *Muḥarram*). He ﷺ replied:

يُكَفِّرُ السَّنَةَ الْمَاضِيَةَ.

> 'It erases the sins of the previous year.'[72]

The fast of the day of ʿ*Arafa* (the Ninth of *Dhū al-Hijja*)

For those who are not in the middle of performing Hajj, it is rewardable to fast that day. Abū Qatāda ؓ narrates that the Prophet ﷺ was asked about the fast on the day of ʿ*arafa*. He ﷺ replied:

يُكَفِّرُ السَّنَةَ الْمَاضِيَةَ وَالْبَاقِيَةَ.

> 'It erases the sins of the (whole) year before (that day) and that which is remaining.'[73]

Let's not forget that it is discouraged for those performing Hajj to fast on the ninth of *Dhū al-Ḥijja*, lest it should cause weakness and prevent the active and lively devotion to the rituals at ʿ*Arafa* (such as supplications). Ibn ʿUmar ؓ said, 'I performed the pilgrimage with the

---

[72] Narrated by Muslim in *al-Ṣaḥīḥ*, 2:819 §1162.

[73] Narrated by Muslim in *al-Ṣaḥīḥ*, 2:819 §1162; and al-Tirmidhī in *al-Sunan*, 2:116 §749.

Prophet ﷺ and I noticed that he ﷺ did not fast the day of *ʿArafa*.'[74]

The jurists however, have allowed those who are certain they would not be overwhelmed by such weakness, to fast that day.[75]

The fast of *Ayyām al-Bīḍ* (white days)

The white days refer to the 13th, 14th and 15th of each lunar month. The Shariah praises fasting these 3 days. Abū Qatāda رضي الله عنه reports that the Prophet ﷺ said:

صَوْمُ ثَلَاثَةٍ مِنْ كُلِّ شَهْرٍ وَرَمَضَانَ إِلَى رَمَضَانَ صَوْمُ الدَّهْرِ.

> 'Fasting 3 days every month and fasting one Ramaḍān after the other is like fasting the whole time.'[76]

The fast of the 15th of Shaʿbān

The Holy Prophet ﷺ issued a directive about performing it. ʿAlī رضي الله عنه reports that the Prophet ﷺ said:

> 'Stand up in prayer (keep up for worship) when the 15th night of Shaʿbān arrives and keep fast the following day. I affirm that Allah ﷻ continues to proclaim, 'Is there anybody who seeks forgiveness so that I forgive him; Is there anyone who seeks provision so that I provide for him; Is there anyone who asks for his need so that I grant him his need; anyone ... anyone ...' until the dawn breaks.'[77]

---

[74] Narrated by al-Tirmidhī in *al-Sunan*, 2:117 §751.

[75] Al-Kāsānī, *Badāʾiʿ al-Ṣānāʾiʿ*, 2:79.

[76] Narrated by Muslim in *al-Ṣaḥīḥ*, 2:819 §1162.

[77] Narrated by al-Bayhaqī in *Shuʿab al-Īmān*, 3:379 §3822.

Q.36. WHAT DOES *AL-NAFL* FAST MEAN?

A: The fasts that are neither obligatory nor imperative are called supererogatory (*al-nafl*) fasts. They earn you reward if you observe them, but do not incur any divine displeasure if you do not observe them.

THE SIX FASTS OF *SHAWWĀL*

Abū Ayyūb al-Anṣārī ◈ narrated the words of the Prophet ◈ as follows:

مَنْ صَامَ رَمَضَانَ ثُمَّ أَتْبَعَهُ سِتًّا مِنْ شَوَّالٍ، كَانَ كَصِيَامِ الدَّهْرِ.

'Whoever fasted the month of Ramaḍān followed by six fasts from Shawwāl, it would be as if he has fasted the whole year.'[78]

THE FAST ON MONDAYS AND THURSDAYS

Abū Hurayra ◈ relates that the Prophet ◈ said:

تُعْرَضُ الأَعْمَالُ يَوْمَ الإِثْنَيْنِ وَالْخَمِيسِ، فَأُحِبُّ أَنْ يُعْرَضَ عَمَلِي وَأَنَا صَائِمٌ.

'Deeds are presented (to the court of Allah) on Mondays and Thursdays. I love to be in the state of fasting when my deeds are presented there.'[79]

Q.37. WHAT ARE *AL-ḤARĀM* FASTS?

A: The holy Prophet ◈ has forbidden fasting on five days of the year. These include ʿĪd al-Fiṭr, ʿĪd al-Aḍḥā, *ayyām al-tashrīq* and the three days just following the tenth of Dhū al-Ḥijja. Abū Saʿīd al-Khudrī ◈ narrates:

نَهَى رَسُولُ الله ﷺ عَنْ صِيَامِ يَوْمَيْنِ: يَوْمِ الْفِطْرِ وَيَوْمِ الأَضْحَى.

---

[78] Narrated by Muslim in *al-Ṣaḥīḥ*, 2:882 §1164.
[79] Narrated by al-Tirmidhī in *al-Sunan*, 2:114 §747.

> 'Allah's Messenger ﷺ has forbidden fasting on two days; the day of *al-Fiṭr* and the day of *al-Aḍḥā*.'[80]

About the days of *al-tashrīq*, Nabītha ؓ reports that the Prophet ﷺ said:

> '*Ayyām al-tashrīq* are days of eating and drinking.'[81]

Q.38. What are *al-Makrūh* (disapproved) fasts?

A: There are days on which Shariah disapproves fasting. We mention them here.

The Saturday fast

ʿAbd Allāh b. Busr ؓ reported his sister to have said that the Prophet ﷺ said,

> 'Do not fast on Saturdays except what has been obligated upon you (in Ramaḍān). If one would not find anything other than a piece of bark of a tree or a peel of grape to break the fast (on a Saturday if one has resolved to fast) he should chew it.'[82]

Imam al-Tirmidhī states that this tradition is *ḥasan* (fair) and the disapproval mentioned here means that one is not allowed to specify Saturday for fasting. Giving Saturday a special religious respect, is part of Jewish ritual.

---

[80] Narrated by Abū Dawūd in *al-Sunan*, 2:314 §2417.
[81] Narrated by Muslim in *al-Ṣaḥīḥ*, 2:800 §1141.
[82] Narrated by al-Tirmidhī in *al-Sunan*, 2:112 §744.

Fasting the *ʿĀshūrāʾ* day alone

Fasting on the tenth of Muḥarram alone, without including either the ninth or eleventh of Muḥarram along with it.

Fasting Friday alone

Fasting on Fridays is disapproved of unless one fasts on the Thursday or Saturday along with it or it happens to fall into your routine. For example, if you fast on the tenth of every month and that happens to be on a Friday. Abū Hurayra ﵁ narrates that the Prophet ﷺ said,

> 'Let one of you not fast on a Friday unless he also fasts one day prior or after it.'[83]

Fasting on *Nawroz*[84]

This is the name of the pre-Islamic Iranian new year's day—the Zoroastrian religion gave it religious respect and spiritual significance. Muslims are not allowed to fast on this day unless, of course, it falls on your routine fasting day.

Without the permission of the husband

A woman is not allowed to keep an optional fast without her husband's permission. Abū Hurayra ﵁ narrates that the Prophet ﷺ said:

---

[83] Narrated by al-Tirmidhī in *al-Sunan*, 2:111 §743.

[84] *Nawroz* is a Persian word (*naw* means 'new' and *roz* means 'day'). *Nowruz* marks the first day of spring and the beginning of the year in Iranian calendar. It is celebrated on the day of the astronomical vernal equinox, which usually occurs on March 21 or the previous/following day depending on where it is observed.

لَا تَصُومُ الْمَرْأَةُ وَزَوْجُهَا شَاهِدٌ يَوْمًا مِنْ غَيْرِ شَهْرِ رَمَضَانَ إِلَّا بِإِذْنِهِ.

'A woman should not keep a fast other than that of Ramaḍān in the presence of her husband without his permission.'[85]

Q.39. What is the fast of David?

A: If you keep fast every alternate day for the whole year, it is called the fast of David as Prophet David ﷺ used to fast this way. ʿAbd Allāh b. ʿAmr ؓ narrates that the Prophet ﷺ said:

إِنَّ أَحَبَّ الصِّيَامِ إِلَى اللهِ تَعَالَى صِيَامُ دَاوُدَ ؛ وَكَانَ يَصُومُ يَوْمًا وَيُفْطِرُ يَوْمًا.

'Allah loves the fast of David the most. He would fast every second day.'[86]

Q.40. What supplications are we supposed to read at the time of pre-dawn meal and fast breaking? Have they been transmitted to us in hadith?

A: We should read the following words when we keep fast.

وَبِصَومِ غَدٍ نَوَيْتُ مِنْ شَهْرِ رَمَضَانَ.

'I have intended to keep the fast of Ramaḍān tomorrow.'

---

[85] Narrated by al-Tirmidhī in *al-Sunan*, 2:142 §782.

[86] Narrated by Muslim in *al-Ṣaḥīḥ*, 2:816 §1159.

What we need to keep in mind here is that no such wording has been mentioned in any hadith. Basically, the intention of the heart is the important thing here. Intention stands for the solemn resolution of the heart, to perform some act of worship. As a term of Shariah, it means 'to intend to gain Allah's proximity through any particular action'.

The intention in prayer, fasting, obligatory alms-due, pilgrimage and other acts of worship is in the heart; not its verbal expression. Since we live in a time of spiritual heedlessness, the verbal assertion helps bring our intention together with our deeds at the appropriate time. Since Islam accepts any unforbidden act that supports a righteous deed as an act of righteousness, it will also be recorded as an additional righteous deed to assert it with the tongue. It earns you reward and gains you blessings. That is why hadith-scholars and Islamic law have regarded by-the-tongue assertion accompanying the commencement of a righteous deed, as a laudable innovation.[87]

For fast breaking, on the other hand, different words have appeared in different narrations. Muʿādh b. Zuhra, for example, narrates that the Prophet ﷺ would read the following words at the time of fast breaking:

اَللّٰهُمَّ لَكَ صُمْتُ وَعَلَى رِزْقِكَ أَفْطَرْتُ.

> 'O Allah! I kept fast for your sake and I break fast with your provision.'[88]

Some books of hadith have added the following words:

وَعَلَيْكَ تَوَكَّلْتُ.

---

[87] Mullā ʿAlī al-Qārī, *Mirqāt al-Mafātīḥ*, 2:304.

[88] Narrated by Abū Dawūd in *al-Sunan*, 2:294 §2385.

'And I placed my trust in you.'

Some other hadiths also include the following words:

فَتَقَبَّلْ مِنِّي، إِنَّكَ أَنْتَ السَّمِيْعُ الْعَلِيْمُ.

'So, please! Accept it from me for you are All-Hearing and All-Knowing.'

In his *Commentary: Mirqāt al-Mafātīḥ*, on the book of hadith, *Mishkāt al-Maṣābiḥ*, Mullā ʿAlī al-Qārī has discussed these hadiths. He concludes that the additional words 'and I believed in You' (*wa bika āmantu*) are absolutely acceptable, despite not having been transmitted in any known hadith, as the addition of words in supplication of this nature is allowed in the Shariah. This addition is like that made by people, of their accord, in *al-talbiya* during pilgrimage.

In the light of the above discussion, we can read the following supplication at the time of fast breaking:

اَللّٰهُمَّ إِنِّي لَكَ صُمْتُ وَبِكَ آمَنْتُ وَعَلَيْكَ تَوَكَّلْتُ وعَلَى رِزْقِكَ أَفْطَرْتُ.

'O Allah! I kept fast for Your sake; did believe in You; placed my trust in You; and completed (i.e., broke) the fast with the provision You have granted.'

Q.41. How does Shariah view the act of back-biting, telling lies, and indecent talk while fasting?

A: In the light of the Shariah, back-biting, lying and indecent talk is not allowed in any condition. While fasting the level of disapproval grows even higher, for these actions violate the whole purpose of fasting.

Keeping a person hungry and thirsty is not the objective of obligating fasting. It rather aims at training a person to restrain oneself from sensual pleasures and evil deeds which include back-biting, lying and indecency of (mind and) word. Take a look at the following hadiths:

1. The Prophet ﷺ said,

> 'If a person does not stop telling lies (despite keeping fast), then Allah ﷻ does not need him to trouble himself with hunger and thirst.'[89]

2. Anas ؓ narrates that the Prophet ﷺ once commanded people to fast and told them not to break their fast without his permission. People did so. At dusk, a person came and requested the permission for breaking the fast after telling the Prophet ﷺ that he had been fasting all day long. The Prophet ﷺ granted him permission. Another person came and asked permission for breaking the fast for two female servants who had been fasting all day long. The holy Prophet ﷺ avoided him at first and then said, 'How could those who have been eating dead human's flesh[90] all day, be considered fasters. If they really think they have been fasting, tell them to vomit *(the truth of their fast will appear to them).*' When they did so, they vomited clots of blood. The person returned to the Prophet ﷺ and told him what he saw. The holy Prophet ﷺ responded, 'If they had died with that blood still inside their bodies, they would be the fuel of Hell-fire.'[91]

3. According to Abū Hurayra's report, the holy Prophet ﷺ narrated that Allah ﷻ said,

---

[89] Narrated by al-Bukhārī in *al-Ṣaḥīḥ*, 2:673 §1804.

[90] This is a Qur'ānic analogy of back-biting. [Qur'ān, *al-Ḥujurāt*, 49:12]

[91] Narrated by al-Ṭayālisī in *al-Musnad*, 1:282 §2107.

> 'Each deed of a human being is for himself except for fasting. It is specifically for Me and only I shall reward it. Fasting is a shield. While fasting, a person should not speak indecently. If somebody swears at him or tries to quarrel with him, he should just respond, 'I am fasting."[92]

These hadiths clearly show that lying, back-biting and indecent talk become more serious transgressions while fasting. The reason for this is that it nullifies the purpose of fasting, thus leaving the one fasting unable to collect the fruits of his hard work and in total deprivation of blessings he is meant to extract from his fast.

Q.42. What are the benefits of fasting?

A: Not only is fasting a source of strength for the soul, it also holds numerous benefits both religious and non-religious and the disclosure of a great number of secrets, which Allah ﷻ does not make available to anybody other than those who fast. We mention some of them below:

1. Piety

Allah ﷻ states:

﴿يَٰٓأَيُّهَا ٱلَّذِينَ ءَامَنُواْ كُتِبَ عَلَيۡكُمُ ٱلصِّيَامُ كَمَا كُتِبَ عَلَى ٱلَّذِينَ مِن قَبۡلِكُمۡ لَعَلَّكُمۡ تَتَّقُونَ﴾

> *O Believers! Fasting is prescribed for you as it was prescribed for the people before you, so that you may become pious.*[93]

Fasting has been prescribed for us as it was for the communities prior to us, in order to make us pious. So, the objective behind enjoining fasting is to initiate the essence of piety in human beings. Thus, it illuminates the

---

[92] Narrated by al-Bukhārī in *al-Ṣaḥīḥ*, 2:673 §1805.

[93] Qur'ān, *al-Baqara*, 2:183.

heart and soul with the light of spiritual blessings. If the piety obtained through fasting is appropriately used, it can potentially introduce a complete shift in the inner universe of the one fasting, which will change his life altogether.

A rather deeper study of the Qur'ān and hadith discloses that piety, which apparently may only help you avoid the forbidden, when coupled with fasting, indeed gives you enough control to restrain yourself to the vicinity of nice and permissible things which you are generally allowed to enjoy.

One month of compulsory training in self-restraint every year is meant to increase the passion for distinguishing between permissible and forbidden, to the extent of settling the rest of the life of the one fasting on righteousness. As a result, the person submits to the will of Allah ﷻ and protects himself from any forbidden impressions.

2. Training in Patience and Gratitude

Patience requires that a person forbear from involving his tongue in wailing and groaning, if lacking or losing a blessing. *Al-Ṣawm* would like to install the one fasting at an even higher station of piety; namely *al-shukr* (gratitude). It wants to promote a state where the holder does not know a wrinkle in the forehead, dejection in the mind or even sadness at heart in cases of tribulation, turbulence and lacking or losing a blessing. Such a person would rather offer gratitude to his Lord, while facing every hardship and harshness with earnest manliness and a smiling face.

In this regard, the mention of two men of spiritual accomplishment seems useful. They happened to meet after a long absence. Each of them asked the other how he was and what his 'state' was. One of them said that his 'state' was such that he gave thanks to Allah if he had received a blessing, or else he would remain patient. The other person said that this was not much. Such would be the state of the dogs in his town. If the owner gave them something to eat they would go around his feet wagging their tails in gratitude. If he does not give the dogs anything, they will still remain faithful and will not go out to find another master. Then he said, 'Our condition is such that we distribute amongst Allah's servants if He gives us something and remain grateful to Him if He does not.' This is why Allah ﷻ, in one of the verses regarding fasting, said,

﴿وَلَعَلَّكُمْ تَشْكُرُونَ﴾

And that you may become grateful.[94]

3. ALTRUISM

A person goes through hunger and thirst during the span of the fast. This gives birth to a feeling of selflessness and sacrifice. He practically becomes aware of the agonies and pains of the indigent classes of human society and those caught in straitened circumstances, by literally going through hunger pangs himself. Indeed, Allah ﷻ wants His affluent servants to be aware of the really unfortunate conditions of paupers and wretched people, those who can barely afford to keep their body and soul together. Thus, we improve the passion for serving the anguished and broken humanity, so as to accentuate the true Islamic society which finds its basis in immortal human values of mutual love, regard, sympathy and philanthropic affability. The awakening of this sensitivity is the inevitable result of fasting. A lack of this senstitivity, on the other hand, shows a completely soulless custom of fasting. Iqbāl said:

---

[94] Qurʾān, *al-Baqara*, 2:185.

روح چوں رفت از صلوة وسلام
فرد ناہموار وملت بے امام

When the soul leaves the body of *salāt* and *salām*, the individual is rendered unworthy and the nation guideless.

4. Self-purification

Fasting purifies the human lower self, heart and soul from every kind of spiritual pollution. The human body is made of matter. In order for it to survive, it has to be provided for with dietary and other material needs. The soul is a subtle existence. Its flourishing depends upon keeping control over material indulgences and forsaking sensual pleasures. Both the body and soul seek their nourishment in measures in opposite directions. Fasting brings the material forces under control, by keeping the body away from food and other matters, and this makes the soul subtler and healthier. The more the servant gets liberated from the clutches of voluptuous desires, the more his soul attains dominance over his body. The relation of the soul and body is that of a bird and its cage. As soon as the bird of the soul finds an opening in the cage of the body, its inclination to flight takes over and it seizes the opportunity to liberate itself from the bonds of the body and enjoys its flight.

A continuous practice of fasting and spiritual endeavor accelerates the process of self-purification. This renders the soul more and more subtle, pure, healthy and powerful. Some perfectly devout personages with inspired knowledge are granted a power that outstrips the vastness and depth of the physical universe around them.

5. Acquisition of Divine pleasure

The prime objective of fasting and the climax of human success aimed through it are to travel through all the spiritual stations and achieve the station of Allah's good pleasure. If we linger here for a moment and reflect upon the meaning of 'Allah's pleasure' as to what it is that a human being could be granted through fasting, it intensifies the feeling of its significance. In comparison with the unique favour of Allah's pleasure, all other blessings are indeed tiny and worthless.

Fasting is a unique practice whose remunerations and reward are left between Allah and His servant. And there is no scale to measure divine pleasure.

Q.43. What is the difference between the fast of 'prominent servants' and that of others?

A: As there is always a hierarchy in every sphere of life, as well as difference of social status in human societies, people in their religious practices and spiritual grades of proximity to Allah are different too. The act of fasting for this reason, can be of two kinds:

1. The fast of Allah's ordinary servants
2. The fast of Allah's prominent servants

The fast of ordinary servants

The first type is that of ordinary people. They are the ones whose fast is no more than a custom in their life. They are not really mindful of the manners and conditions of fasting. According to the teachings of the Holy Prophet Muhammad ﷺ, the majority of these do not receive anything but hunger pangs and a raging thirst. Those who remain in deliberate opposition to divine commandments and recommendations while keeping fast, by continuing to lie, back-bite, deceive and commit other wicked acts as usual, their acts of fasting and prayer are soulless bodies and can earn them neither blessings nor spiritual favours.

Such fasting cannot positively leave any beneficial impression upon the members of the *Umma*.

The fast of prominent servants

The second type of fast is that of prominent worshipful servants, who comply with the commandments of Allah and keep themselves from minor and major sins. Fasting creates the quality of piety so that their lives embody the words of the Qur'ān, *'So that you become pious'*.[95] By the favours of piety, their lives experience a complete shift. They now are accustomed to a clear distinction between permissible and forbiden.

According to the words of the Prophet ﷺ, the fast that they have taken up for their lives becomes a shield between them and the torment of Hell-fire:

> 'Fasting is a shield between you and the fire of Hell like a shield you have while fighting (the enemy in the middle of battlefield).'[96]

The above discussion shows the difference between the fast of ordinary servants and those of prominent worshipful service. It concludes that the fast of ordinary people is confined to the custom of eating pre-dawn meal and breaking fast, whereas the fast of the prominent servants, based on their spiritual endeavour and austerity, leads them to the beatific vision of the divine countenance. For the latter aspire to nothing less than the good pleasure of Allah ﷻ, the vision of the divine countenance and the favour of the vision of the bright face of the Prophet ﷺ.

---

[95] Qur'ān, *al-Baqara*, 2:183.

[96] Narrated by Ibn Mājah in *al-Sunan*, 2:305 §1639.

Q.44. Does fasting influence every person equally?

A: Fasting does not leave the same spiritual and physical impression upon everybody. Despite the blessings and prominence attached to fasting, the equal acquisition of its favours by everybody is not possible. The holy Prophet ﷺ said:

> 'There are a great many people who fast but only get hunger and thirst out of their fast. There are a great many people who offer prayer at night but only get (the discomfort of) night vigil out of it.'[97]

Whoever lives his life to abide by the commands of Allah ﷻ, enjoins the good and prohibits the evil, remains firmly faithful with all its conditions and prerequisites, and does not become unmindful of self-evaluation will receive glad tidings.

Abū Hurayra ؓ reported that the Prophet ﷺ said,

> 'Whoever fasts [on] Ramaḍān with faith and the intention of reward, will have his previous sins forgiven. Whoever performs *al-qiyām* of Ramaḍān with faith and the intention of its reward, will have his previous sins forgiven. Whoever stands up in worshipful service during the Night of Destiny will have his previous sins forgiven.'[98]

The same is true of the physical effects of fasting. They also appear differently on different people. If one person for example, works in an air-conditioned office and another works in the blazing sun all day long, their levels

---

[97] Narrated by Ibn Khuzayma in *al-Ṣaḥīḥ*, 3:242 §1997.

[98] Narrated by al-Bukhārī in *al-Ṣaḥīḥ*, 2:709 §1910.

of dehydration and the intensity of their weakness will be different. Each, likewise, will be granted rewards according to the patience and forbearance he will have observed and the strength of aspiration behind his fast.

Q.45. How can we protect our fast?

A: If the fast is accomplished with all the rulings and manners regarding it in full consideration, then it undoubtedly increases the protection against committing sins. If somebody however, intended to fast and kept himself from food, drink and his wife without safeguarding himself against earning forbidden, back-biting and other sins of the kind, his fast would not earn him the intended blessings or bear him the fruit he should expect, even though his basic obligation will be performed in full view.

Abū ʿUbayda b. al-Jarrāḥ ﷺ narrates that the Prophet ﷺ said:

اَلصَّوْمُ جُنَّةٌ مَا لَمْ يَخْرِقْهَا.

> 'Fast is a shield so long as the faster does not tear it apart.'[99]

Abū Hurayra ﷺ narrates that the Prophet ﷺ said:

مَنْ لَمْ يَدَعْ قَوْلَ الزُّوْرِ وَالْعَمَلَ بِهِ، فَلَيْسَ لِلّٰهِ حَاجَةٌ فِي أَنْ يَدَعَ طَعَامَهُ وَشَرَابَهُ.

> 'Whoever does not leave (stop) telling lies and practising false (while fasting), then (he must know that) Allah does not need his cessation of eating and drinking.'[100]

---

[99] Narrated by al-Nasāʾī in *al-Sunan*, 1:167 §2233.

[100] Narrated by al-Bukhārī in *al-Ṣaḥīḥ*, 2:673 §1804.

The cessation of eating, drinking or sexual relations does not perfect the fast. The state of fasting rather includes ceasing to commit indecency (of word and action), reprehensible and objectionable deeds and other kinds of sins. The hadiths prove that the one fasting must also:

- Protect his tongue from lying, back-biting, slandering, calumny and indecent talk.
- Protect his eyes form seeing everything whose seeing is condemnable and disapproved of or whose sight makes him unmindful of Allah's remembrance.
- Protect his ears from listening to anything that is a sin to listen to. If a gathering is involved with back-biting or other sinful talk, advise them to desist. If they do not stop, leave the gathering as the Prophet ﷺ has told us that both the back-biter and the one who listens are partners in sin.
- Not eat at fast breaking time more than enough to tighten the belly and just keep it relaxed.
- Keep the heart between hope and fear about whether the fast has been accepted or not after being completed, but not be disappointed in the mercy of Allah.
- Protect the limbs from relative sins is safeguarding the fast.

Q.46. Which two delights is the one fasting granted?

A: In contrast to other acts of worship, fasting is unique for earning the one fasting two delights at the same time. Abū Hurayra narrates that the Prophet ﷺ said:

لِلصَّائِمِ فَرْحَتَانِ يَفْرَحُهُمَا: إِذَا أَفْطَرَ فَرِحَ، وَإِذَا لَقِيَ رَبَّهُ فَرِحَ بِصَوْمِهِ.

> 'The faster has two delights to enjoy them both. He is delighted when he breaks his fast [the delight of fast breaking] and he will be delighted [the delight of beatific vision of Allah's countenance] for his fast when he will meet his Lord.'[101]

Q.47. Which door of Paradise is only for those who fast?

A: There are eight doors to enter Paradise, each of which is specific to a particular act of worship. If someone sincerely performs one of those deeds abundantly and enjoys it most, he will be invited to enter Paradise through the door specific to that deed. *Al-Rayyān* is the door amongst those doors which is specific to fasting and only those who fast will enter Paradise through that door. The holy Prophet ﷺ said, according to the narration of Sahl b. Saʿd ؓ:

إِنَّ فِي الْجَنَّةِ بَابًا يُقَالُ لَهُ الرَّيَّانُ، يَدْخُلُ مِنْهُ الصَّائِمُوْنَ يَوْمَ الْقِيَامَةِ، لاَ يَدْخُلُ مِنْهُ أَحَدٌ غَيْرُهُمْ، يُقَالُ: أَيْنَ الصَّائِمُوْنَ؟ فَيَقُوْمُوْنَ، لاَ يَدْخُلُ مِنْهُ أَحَدٌ غَيْرُهُمْ، فَإِذَا دَخَلُوْا أُغْلِقَ، فَلَمْ يَدْخُلْ مِنْهُ أَحَدٌ.

> 'There is a door in Paradise called *al-rayyān*. On the Day of Judgement, only the fasters will be invited to enter it and none other will be allowed through it. A call will be made for the fasters whereupon they will stand up and only they will be allowed through it. Then it will be closed, once they will have entered, no one else will be able to enter it.'[102]

---

[101] Narrated by al-Bukhārī in *al-Ṣaḥīḥ*, 2:673 §1805.

[102] Narrated by al-Bukhārī in *al-Ṣaḥīḥ*, 2:671 §1797.

The word *al-rayyān* means 'verdant, luxuriant, succulent, well-watered and well-irrigated'. Hadith-scholar, Mullā ʿAlī al-Qārī discusses the reason why it is called *al-rayyān*. He concludes that it may have been so named because it is verdant for many streams run in it and it is covered with fresh greenery that boasts an abundance of succulent fruits and eye-catching flowers. Another possible reason for so naming it is its quality of satiating the thirsty and refreshing the weary so as never to lose that bright freshness again.[103]

It is not confined to the fast of Ramaḍān. Those who offer optional fasts all year round also deserve it.

Q.48. What are the spiritual benefits of fasting?

A: The internal and spiritual benefits of fasting are as follows:

- Fasting is a well-tested prescription for weak souls and ill hearts. Its practice makes strength and freshness available for the soul. It initiates an inclination towards good deeds and instils disgust for wickedness.
- Fasting enables the one fasting to restrain himself to Allah's limits and cast himself into the frame of divine commandments. This helps him live a successful life.
- Fasting establishes the quality of rectitude in all the matters of religion and this helps the one fasting to practice the *Dīn* firmly and safeguard himself against deviation.
- Fasting establishes the quality of self-purification and internal cleansing.
- The one fasting will be granted a blessing above his best expectations [that is the vision of beatific glory of the

[103] Mullā ʿAlī al-Qārī, *Mirqāt al-Mafātīḥ*, 4:230.

Lord]. Martyrs will wish to be given life and lose it again and again in the cause of Allah just for its re-acquisition.

- There is no better brightener than fasting to burnish the heart and soul and render the inner self free of all types of pollution. Fasting protects one against sins and Hell fire.

- Allah ﷻ remunerates each deed from ten times to seven hundred times except for fasting. Only Allah ﷻ knows what that reward is and He will give it Himself. Abū Hurayra ؓ narrates that the Prophet ﷺ said:

كُلُّ عَمَلِ ابْنِ آدَمَ يُضَاعَفُ ، اَلْحَسَنَةُ بِعَشْرِ أَمْثَالِهَا إِلَى سَبْعِمِائَةِ ضِعْفٍ إِلَى مَا شَاءَ اللهُ. يَقُوْلُ اللهُ تَعَالَى: إِلَّا الصَّوْمَ فَإِنَّهُ لِي، وَأَنَا أَجْزِي بِهِ.

> 'The strength of each human deed's reward is increased from ten times to seven hundred times to as many times as Allah ﷻ wills per righteous deed, except for the act of fasting. Allah ﷻ declares: It is only for Me and only I shall award its recompense.'[104]

Q.49. What are the physical/medical benefits of fasting?

A: Allah ﷻ states in the Qur'ān:

(وَأَن تَصُومُوا۟ خَيْرٌ لَّكُمْ إِن كُنتُمْ تَعْلَمُونَ)

> *And your fasting is better for you, if you understand.*[105]

If we study the facts stated in this verse from a medical perspective, we find that fasting is not only an act of

---

[104] Narrated by Ibn Mājah in *al-Sunan*, 2:305 §1638.

[105] Qur'ān, *al-Baqara*, 2:184.

worshipful service to the Lord Almighty; it is also a benefit for the health of the human body. The experts on the subject hold that fasting does not cause weakness. It only lengthens the time span between two meals. It does not prevent the acquisition of the calories and water needed for a healthy body every 24 hours. It has also been witnessed that those fasting tend to increase the consumption of proteins and carbohydrates during Ramaḍān. In view of the average eating routine of those fasting, we can easily deduce that the calories collected during any given 24 hours of Ramaḍān amount to a higher degree than required. We also know very well that the human body tends to make up for the calories needed but not taken in, in case somebody does so, by burning up the surplus energy stored in the body. Below, we make mention of some of the medical benefits of fasting.

• Fasting provides a month of proper rest for the digestive system, something which has an amazing positive effect upon the liver, which gets tired because it also has duties to perform other than helping with the digestive system. Fasting gives it rest from four to six hours a day, something that is impossible without fasting. We all know that even one-tenth of a gram of food, the moment it enters our stomach, would set the whole digestive system to work, with the liver fully involved as an essential part. In order to help the liver work better and for a longer time, as the experts in the scientific and medical study of the human body would argue, it has to have this break at least once a year.

• While fasting, the amount of blood decreases and this provides the heart with some extremely useful rest. The reduction of intercellular liquid makes the work of the cells quite tranquil. The epithelia which are responsible for the constant draining of harmful moisture out of the body, can also take some rest during the fast. Fasting also reduces the diastolic pressure upon the muscles of the heart, which allows it a great deal of relaxation. This is very important; particularly in our times when the peculiar circumstances of the modern lifestyle have resulted in a great deal of tension for the human being.

- Lungs cleanse the blood directly, so they receive the positive effects of fasting directly too. Fasting prevents the clotting of the blood in the lungs and dissolves it if it has occurred, by cleansing the bronchioles and alveoli. We must also keep in mind that while fasting the lungs also accelerate the cleansing of the blood, something which leaves its positive effects upon the whole body.

- Fasting also helps to produce blood in the body. When dietary elements come down to a certain level, the bone marrow makes its movement efficient. This, along with the liver having had enough rest and being at ease to work, helps people with a blood deficiency produce more blood easily.

- The number of red corpuscles in the blood is greater than the white. The experts say that body temperature falls while fasting. When hunger is intense, the body tends to return to its original state. After breaking the fast when food is consumed, body temperature rises to an extent. After keeping fast, the process of cleansing the blood starts. A study of those inflicted with anemia has revealed an increase in the amount of red corpuscles. According to one study, only twelve days' consecutive fasting increased the number of red corpuscles from 500,000 to 3,600,000.

Q.50. What are the benefits of collective fast breaking?

A: Jābir ﷺ narrates that the Prophet ﷺ said:

> 'The food of one person suffices two; that of two persons suffices four; and that of four persons suffices eight.'[106]

Collective fast breaking eliminates class discrimination and instils an environment of love, affection, altruism and sacrifice. At the same time, it earns those who organise such events the good pleasure of Allah ﷻ and His beloved Messenger ﷺ.

The holy Prophet ﷺ said, 'Ramaḍān is a month when provision is increased. Whoever arranges *al-ifṭār* for a faster gets his sins forgiven and his neck liberated from the Fire. He is also granted the full reward of the fast of that faster without any reduction in his reward.' The Companions ؓ raised their concern that not all amongst them could afford to arrange a proper *al-ifṭār* for others fasting. The Prophet ﷺ responded, 'Even if somebody could manage to have another faster break his fast with one sip of milk, one piece of date or one sip of water, he will be granted the reward promised.'[107]

Q.51. What is the wisdom behind breaking your fast with dates?

A: Dates are a type of food full of energy. Fasting keeps a person hungry all day long; as a result the body needs a diet that restores energy. Dates are a suitable source to make up for the loss of energy and for sugar deficiency. Allah ﷻ has mentioned dates in the Qur'ān at different places and from different perspectives. Hadiths also mention its dietary benefits.

Anas ؓ narrates that holy Prophet ﷺ would break his fast with a few succulent dates just before offering *al-Maghrib* prayer. If they were not available, he ﷺ would

---

[106] Narrated by Muslim in *al-Ṣaḥīḥ*, 3:1630 §2059.

[107] Narrated by Ibn Khuzayma in *al-Ṣaḥīḥ*, 3:192 §1887.

take dry ones. If they were not available either, he ﷺ would take a few sips of water.[108]

This practice of the holy Prophet ﷺ does have its scientific implications. If we break our fast with a few dates, the sucrose immediately gets absorbed with the saliva and is converted to glucose, which helps the body restore temperature and energy. As opposed to this if we take hot, spicy, oily or fried food, they increase the acidity in the stomach causing heartburn and continual thirst. They also dissolve digestive enzymes and so weaken the inner walls of the stomach and cause a slight increase in temperature. Fast breaking with dates does not cause heaviness of the stomach. Nor does it increase hydrochloric acid in the stomach and thus increase temperature. Dates also contain numerous other medically proven benefits. For example, they protect against diseases involving phlegm and cold; help with memory improvement; help the heart and kidneys with their work; help counter anaemia; and are useful in treating respiratory problems, particularly asthma.

The Arabs have an old saying: there are as many reasons to use a date as there are days in a year.

Q.52. What role does fasting play in controlling diabetes?

A: It plays a considerable role in controlling the sugar level. There is the general perception that a diabetic person must experience unbearable conditions if he fasts. Some people are overwhelmed by the assumption that fasting will bring the sugar level or water level below the necessary level, something that is not the actual position. Such an occurrence is only possible when the diabetes is

---

[108] Narrated by al-Tirmidhī in *al-Sunan*, 2:73 §696.

severe and the patient is already in a critical condition; a situation for which the Shariah has already provided concession. As Allah ﷻ said in the Qur'ān:

﴿وَمَن كَانَ مَرِيضًا أَوْ عَلَىٰ سَفَرٍ فَعِدَّةٌ مِّنْ أَيَّامٍ أُخَرَ ۗ يُرِيدُ ٱللَّهُ بِكُمُ ٱلْيُسْرَ وَلَا يُرِيدُ بِكُمُ ٱلْعُسْرَ﴾

He who is ill or on a journey should complete the count by (fasting an equal number of) other days. Allah desires ease for you and does not desire hardship for you.[109]

According to the opinions held by the experts on the subject, non-fasting people have their sugar levels subject to increase and decrease, while those of people fasting tends to remain normal, against all the odds of public perception. The reason for this is that fasting does not introduce any new problem to the patient. Moreover, if fasting is observed as a routine all year round (like three days a month or once or twice a week or something similar), it not only controls the sugar level but also helps fight against the weakness caused by irregular ups and downs in sugar levels. Fasting also helps the immune system of a diabetic to a reasonable extent, in fighting against the problems caused by diabetes itself, such as blindness, swelling of the brain, troubles regarding the kidneys and cataracts.

Q.53. Does fasting help against obesity?

A: Yes it does, provided that we remember the following divine command.

﴿كُلُوا۟ وَٱشْرَبُوا۟ وَلَا تُسْرِفُوٓا۟﴾

Eat and drink but do not spend extravagantly.[110]

---

[109] Qur'ān, *al-Baqara*, 2:185.

[110] Qur'ān, *al-Aʿrāf*, 7:31.

This verse advises us not to eat excessively. If the one fasting abides by this directive, while he takes pre-dawn meal and breaks fast, he can manage to lose weight. Obesity is caused by the increase of oily substances in our body. Such people have an increased amount of fatty acids. Particles of cholesterol are also increased.

People with this problem always find it hard to get rid of it, regardless if they adopt some diet or not. Overeating invites other diseases. This is why it is also called 'the mother of diseases'. In this disease, the person afflicted needs to keep adipose cells under control. Fasting is the best means to do so. By changing the whole day's routine, the month of Ramaḍān proves a refresher course in the practice of consecutive fasting. It trains one to restrain oneself from sensual pleasures and remain patient in the face of hunger and thirst. By providing a training course in dietary matters, Ramaḍān introduces a positive and hopeful change in human fatty acid.

Q.54. What role does fasting play in the prevention of cancer?

A: According to the research conducted recently, fasting helps in the prevention of cancer. It stops cancer cells from proliferating. While fasting, the level of glucose falls. The body needs glucose like a machine needs fuel; the absence of glucose forces the body to switch to the surplus fats stored in the body. The process gives birth to ketone bodies which brings an end to the breaking of protein molecules into small particles. Cancer cells thrive on these particles of protein. Their reduced production while fasting helps prevent cancer.

Q.55. Is fasting helpful in quitting smoking?

A: Yes it is. Every right-minded person can differentiate between good and bad, but many fall victim to dangerous enjoyments for the reason of lacking resolve. Fasting endows a person with patience, forbearance and strong resolve. Friedrich Wilhelm Nietzsche has written a book *The Will to Power*. In the way of establishing a determined personality, he counts fasting amongst the most basic components. He gives examples of those who manage to quit smoking through the means of fasting. It is common knowledge that one who fasts does not smoke from dawn to dusk. That is up to 13 or 14 hours a day (or even more in some places). In this way, discipline takes place in the temperament of the one who fasts and this can help him quit smoking for good.

Q.56. What lessons can we extract from fasting?

A: Fasting gives the lesson of obedience to Allah ﷾, self-purification, brotherhood and sympathy. For example, a person prohibits himself food, drink and other desires from dawn to dusk, which are lawful at other times, but may be obligated in some situations. Fasting teaches us what it means to exert true worshipful service to Allah. It firmly settles in us the point that obedience to Allah is the main thing. The only certificate for something to be right or wrong is Allah's word.

In the same way, fasting also makes us feel the agonies of poverty and wretchedness. Remaining foodless for hours makes the one fasting feel for those who go through this every day of their lives. So, the one who fasts contributes the best he can to reduce their agonies and remove their pains. This is the very reason Muslims have been described as a single soul, whose whole body shares the feeling of pain affecting one of the parts of the body, such as the eye or ear, etc.

4. Rulings about the Fast Itself

Q.57. Is intention necessary for fasting?

A: Yes. In order for the fast to be valid, intention holds the first importance. Abstaining from food, drink and marital relations, from dawn to dusk, without the intention, cannot be considered fasting. According to three of the schools of Islamic law, one has to make a separate intention for each fast. Our Imam Abū Ḥanīfa holds that the intention for the whole month at the start of Ramaḍān will suffice, if one continues to fast for the whole month without a break.

Q.58. Do we have to say *al-niyya* with the tongue?

A: No. *Al-Niyya* is the name for the heart's intention. If somebody gets up before dawn with the intention of eating pre-dawn meal for fasting the following day and does so, this much would count for him as *al-niyya*. It is however, laudable to utter the words of *al-niyya* founded on the Prophetic practice.

Q.59. Does *al-niyya* of breaking the fast break it?

A: If somebody makes up his mind to break his fast while still fasting, sometime during the day, it will not break his fast. The holy Prophet ﷺ said,

> 'Allah ﷻ has forgiven the thoughts that occur to the hearts of my *Umma*, unless they are said or done.'[111]

Q.60. When does the time of pre-dawn meal end? Are we allowed to eat something after that?

A: The time of pre-dawn meal starts after the first half of the night has passed and ends just a few moments before the break of dawn. Once that time has ended, we are not allowed to eat or drink anything. Zayd b. Thābit ؓ reports that they had their pre-dawn meal with the Prophet ﷺ. After a while, the Prophet ﷺ got up for *al-Fajr* prayer. One of the students asked Zayd how long it was between the end of pre-dawn meal and the call to *al-Fajr* prayer. He replied, 'As long as it takes to recite fifty verses.'[112]

The vast majority of jurists hold that we are allowed to eat if we are not sure whether the dawn has broken or not. Once we are sure of the time, we have to stop eating.

Q.61. Why have we been commanded to take pre-dawn meal late and break fast early?

A: Doing so is a well-emphasised Prophetic practice. The Holy Prophet ﷺ would always eat pre-dawn meal late and break fast early.

ʿAbd Allāh b. Abbās ؓ narrates that the Prophet ﷺ said:

إِنَّا مَعْشَرَ الأَنْبِيَاءِ، أُمِرْنَا أَنْ نُؤَخِّرَ سُحُوْرَنَا وَنُعَجِّلَ فُطُوْرَنَا.

---

[111] Narrated by al-Bukhārī in *al-Ṣaḥīḥ*, 2:894 §2391.

[112] Narrated by al-Bukhārī in *al-Ṣaḥīḥ*, 2:678 §1821.

'We, the group of Prophets, have been commanded to delay pre-dawn meal (towards its later time, just before its end time) and hasten fast breaking (as soon as the time starts, just after the dusk).'[113]

Sahl b. Saʿd ☙ narrates that the Prophet ﷺ said:

لَا يَزَالُ النَّاسُ بِخَيْرٍ مَا عَجَّلُوا الْفِطْرَ.

'The people of my *Umma* will have the goodness (of their fast), as long as they hasten the fast breaking.'[114]

Abū Hurayra ☙ narrates that the Prophet ﷺ said:

إِذَا سَمِعَ أَحَدُكُمُ النِّدَاءَ وَالْإِنَاءُ عَلَى يَدِهِ ، فَلاَ يَضَعُهُ حَتَّى يَقْضِيَ حَاجَتَهُ مِنْهُ.

'When one of you hears the call to prayer while he still has the pot (of food) in his hand, let him not place it back before fulfilling his need from it (finish what he was eating).'[115]

The above-mentioned hadiths show clearly that it is Sunna to delay the pre-dawn meal till its later time and to hasten the breaking of fast to its earliest time. This command covers many points of wisdom. Apart from its spiritual blessings, it helps us stay strong enough to do our routine jobs and prevents the pangs of hunger and the rage of thirst growing to their extreme.

---

[113] Narrated by Ibn Ḥibbān in *al-Ṣaḥīḥ*, 5:67 §1770.

[114] Narrated by Muslim in *al-Ṣaḥīḥ*, 2:771 §1098.

[115] Narrated by Abū Dawūd in *al-Sunan*, 2:292 §2350; and al-Ḥākim in *al-Mustadrak*, 1:323 §740.

Our beloved Prophet ﷺ has advised his *Umma* to take pre-dawn meal, even if it is one sip of water, a piece of date or a few grains of raisins.[116]

The reason for hastening the fast breaking is to avoid the Jewish and Christian practice of waiting for the stars to appear, which causes suspicion of star-worshiping and faith in astrological horoscope reading. The *Umma* will conform to the good by complying strictly to the Sunna and the limits of the Shariah, as long as they delay pre-dawn meal and hasten breaking of fast.

Q.62. What are the disapproved things for the one who fasts?

A: The following things are disapproved of while fasting:

- To chew gum or keep something in the mouth.
- To taste something when it is not necessary to do so. A woman whose husband is peevish and ill-tempered, however, is allowed to taste while cooking with the tip of her tongue.
- To gargle excessively or sniff water excessively when cleaning the nose.
- To gather a lot of saliva in the mouth and then swallow it.
- To lie, back-bite or swear.
- To express agitation and impatience with hunger or thirst.
- To delay the ritual bath until after the break of dawn, if it was obligated earlier.
- To observe consecutive fasts, without a break, outside Ramaḍān, even if it lasts only for two days.

---

[116] Narrated by al-Ṭabarānī in *Musnad al-Shāmiyyīn*, 1:32 §16.

Q.63. What are the rulings of the Shariah regarding *al-qaḍā*ʾ[117] of fasting?

A: There are three positions in this regard:

1. If somebody eats or drinks something while forgetful of his fast (it was just not in his mind at the time of eating or drinking), he is not responsible for any of *al-qaḍā*ʾ or *al-kaffāra.*[118]

2. If somebody eats or drinks while mindful of his fast of Ramaḍān, but he does not have any *al-*ʿ*udhr*,[119] he is responsible for both *al-qaḍā*ʾ and *al-kaffāra*.

3. If somebody eats or drinks while mindful of his fast of Ramaḍān, but he has an *al-*ʿ*udhr* (such as travel or illness), he is only responsible for *al-qaḍā*ʾ and not *al-kaffāra*.

Q.64. Which factors obligate *al-qaḍā*ʾ without *al-kaffāra*?

A: Such things as follows:

- Somebody inserts something in the mouth of the one fasting forcefully and it goes down his throat.
- One is mindful of the fast but swallows some water while gargling.

---

[117] Making up for an omission in religious duties, such as fasting, by repeating it or performing it after its appointed time has gone.

[118] Expiation or atonement for neglected duties, sins of commission or omission is known as *al-kaffāra*, which takes different forms such as prayer, freeing slaves, fasting etc.

[119] An excuse that is acceptable to the Shariah in order to validate a concession for its subjects, regarding acts of commission and omission.

- While mindful of his fast, he causes himself to discharge a mouthful[120] of vomit or vomits less than a mouthful but he swallows or happens to swallow some of it back.
- While mindful of his fast, he swallows a pebble or the stone of a fruit or a piece of soil or a piece of paper.
- To take something like a chickpea or larger stuck in the teeth with the tongue and swallow it. If he takes it out of his mouth and then swallows it, it breaks the fast even if it was smaller than a chickpea.
- To swallow the blood from the gums mixed with saliva if it overwhelms the saliva. Otherwise, it does not break his fast.
- If somebody eats or drinks out of forgetfulness, thus believing his fast has been broken, and then eats or drinks something with that in mind.
- If somebody wakes up late before dawn and eats under the false assumption (for some reason, for example his watch does not work properly and is late) that he has not run out of time yet, which he later finds out was a mistake.
- To break any fast other than Ramaḍān on purpose.
- To break the fast by making the *ifṭār* under the false assumption that dusk has fallen whereas it has not yet.

In all the conditions mentioned above the fast will be broken and only the *qaḍā*ʾ will be obligated.

[120] Mouthful means either an amount too great or with too great a force to keep the mouth shut or to keep it within the mouth without letting any of it out.

Q.65. Should we fast while making the *qaḍā*ʾ of Ramaḍān in succession or with breaks?

A: The *al-qaḍā*ʾ for fasts missed during Ramaḍān is an obligation. As far as the time frame is concerned, the Shariah has provided room and nothing has been specified. It is acceptable both ways: keep them consecutively or spread them out over the rest of the following year.

Q.66. What routine did ʿĀʾisha ﷺ adopt regarding the performance of *al-qaḍā*ʾ fasts of Ramaḍān?

A: She would always make *al-qaḍā*ʾ of Ramaḍān fasts which she had to miss for valid excuse, during Shaʿbān, for the Prophet ﷺ would also fast a lot during this month (although the fast he ﷺ would keep was optional). Abū Salama ﷺ narrates that ʿĀʾisha ﷺ said:

> 'If I had to expiate for the fasts of Ramaḍān, I would be best able to do so during Shaʿbān.'[121]

About the expiation of Ramaḍān fasts, Mother of the Believers ʿĀʾisha ﷺ would never accept a position where she was unable to serve her husband ﷺ because of fasting, whenever he ﷺ had any duty for her. On the basis of this hadith, jurists have deduced that a woman is not allowed to observe optional fast without the permission of her husband.

Q.67. Is it imperative to expiate for an optional fast if one breaks it?

A: There is no *al-qaḍā*ʾ for an optional fast broken for some reason. If somebody, however, breaks an optional

---

[121] Narrated by Muslim in *al-Ṣaḥīḥ*, 2:802 §1146.

fast on purpose and without any valid excuse, *al-qaḍā'* is an obligation. The following hadith explains this:

> ʿĀ'isha ﷺ narrates that Mother of the Believers, Ḥafṣa and she ﷺ kept optional fast. During the fast, they were offered food which they liked and therefore ate it. When the Prophet ﷺ came home, Ḥafṣa ﷺ spoke and said, 'O Allah's Messenger! While we were fasting, we were offered food that we liked and ate (so, what should we do now)?' The Prophet ﷺ said, 'Make *al-qaḍā'* for it some other day.'[122]

Q.68. What is expiation and how is it done?

A: The Shariah has obligated *al-kaffāra* (expiation) to release *al-mukallaf* (the one held responsible and accountable to Allah) from the punishment for his sins in both abodes by omitting them. Expiation generally speaking takes the form of fasting, freeing slaves, feeding or clothing the needy.

Abū Hurayra ﷺ narrates that a person happened to have intercourse with his wife in Ramaḍān while fasting. He then came to the Prophet ﷺ and asked what the ruling was in such a situation. The Prophet ﷺ asked him if he could afford to free a slave. The answer was negative. Then he ﷺ asked if he could keep sixty consecutive fasts. The answer was negative again. Then the Prophet ﷺ said, 'Then feed sixty needy people.'[123]

---

[122] Narrated by al-Tirmidhī in *al-Sunan*, 2:104 §735.

[123] Narrated by Muslim in *al-Ṣaḥīḥ*, 2:783 §1111.

Q.69. What is the atonement for breaking an optional fast?

A: Atonement is only obligated in case of breaking the obligatory fast during Ramaḍān. No other fast be it optional or *al-qaḍā'* of Ramaḍān, requires an obligation of atonement.

Q.70. How can one perform atonement by fasting?

A: In this case one has to fast for two months seriatim, without a break. For example, one starts on the first day of a lunar month and carries on fasting till the end of the following month. If one starts on the 15th of a lunar month, he has to complete that month, carry on for the whole next month and then for the first 14 days of the third month. He has to complete two consecutive lunar months of fasting without a break. The day he takes a break, his atonement is no more. He has to do it anew, from day one again.

However in the case of women, there is one difference. Since they are not allowed to fast during their monthly periods of menstruation, their days of menstrual bleeding will not be taken as break, although those days will not be counted as fasts. They will continue to fast following the day their period ends and complete 60 fasts. In the case of post-natal bleeding, their fast prior to its occurrence is no longer a part of atonement. After the end of bleeding, they will start the fast of atonement anew.

Q.71. What is the amount or quality of the food offered to 60 needy people as expiation?

A: It means to feed a person two belly-full meals a day, for sixty days. Another option is to buy sixty needy people 2 kilograms of wheat each or to give them its retail market price (in the country one lives and according to the currency he uses in his daily life). One can also buy them rice, millet or some other oats/grains with that money (the price of 2 kg of wheat per person for sixty people).

Another point to be kept in mind is that any of those indigent being paid should not be his own dependents, such as his parents, his wife, his grandparents, his children or grandchildren.

Q.72. Can the food of expiation for sixty people be given to one helpless person?

A: If somebody wants to pay the expiation of one or more fasts to one person, he can do so. Similarly, a person can give more than one fast in one instance.

Q.73. What is the ruling about a person who misses a fast of Ramaḍān without a valid excuse?

A: Ramaḍān is a month that holds the special blessings of Allah ﷻ. It is a month when supplications are accepted. There are a great deal of blessings and favours, both worldly and spiritual, which a human being can only acquire through the faithful act of fasting. Unfortunate is the one who deprives himself of Allah's mercy, by not fasting without being excused by the Shariah. A hadith narrated by Abū Hurayra ؓ explains the regrettable and pathetic position of such a person. It states that the Prophet ﷺ said:

مَنْ أَفْطَرَ يَوْمًا مِنْ رَمَضَانَ، مِنْ غَيْرِ رُخْصَةٍ وَلَا مَرَضٍ، لَمْ يَقْضِ عَنْهُ صَوْمُ الدَّهْرِ كُلِّهِ، وَإِنْ صَامَهُ.

> 'Whoever leaves one fast of Ramaḍān without any concession or illness (accepted as a valid excuse by the Shariah), even fasting for his whole life will never be able to make it up for him.'[124]

According to the jurists of the Shariah, if somebody breaks his Ramaḍān fast knowingly, the obligation of both *al-qaḍā'* and *al-kaffāra* will take effect.

Q.74. What is the ruling of the Shariah in case of breaking the Ramaḍān fast for the reason of illness?

A: It is important to break the fast if the one fasting is afflicted with some illness, in the case of which continuing with his fast can lead to death, to worsen his disease or delay its recovery. After the recovery, its *al-qaḍā'* will be obligated. Allah ﷻ states:

(وَمَن كَانَ مَرِيضًا أَوْ عَلَىٰ سَفَرٍ فَعِدَّةٌ مِّنْ أَيَّامٍ أُخَرَ ۗ يُرِيدُ ٱللَّهُ بِكُمُ ٱلْيُسْرَ وَلَا يُرِيدُ بِكُمُ ٱلْعُسْرَ وَلِتُكْمِلُوا۟ ٱلْعِدَّةَ وَلِتُكَبِّرُوا۟ ٱللَّهَ عَلَىٰ مَا هَدَىٰكُمْ وَلَعَلَّكُمْ تَشْكُرُونَ)

> *Therefore, he who witnesses this month must fast it, and he who is ill or on a journey should complete the count by (fasting an equal number of) other days. Allah desires ease for you and does not desire hardship for you so that you complete the prescribed number of fasting days,*

---

[124] Narrated by al-Tirmidhī in *al-Sunan*, 2:93 §723.

and that you glorify Him for the guidance which He has blessed you with, and that you may become grateful.[125]

Q.75. Is it allowed to break the fast for extreme weakness or intense illness?

A: If a severe disease or extreme weakness raises concerns about the possible progression of that disease, or delay its recovery or a significant increase of weakness (which will not allow the one fasting to do his daily job and nobody can take over from him) if the fast is continued to its completion at dusk, the one fasting is allowed to break his fast before dusk. In this case, *al-qaḍāʾ* for that fast is obligated after Ramaḍān.

Q.76. What is *al-fidya*?

A: If somebody is too old to fast for the rest of his life at all or he is afflicted with a disease which is too severe to let him fast for the rest of his life, then he is allowed to leave off fasting and serve a meal to the needy instead. This is known as *al-fidya* (ransom). The number of needy is not specified. Allah ﷻ states:

﴿وَعَلَى ٱلَّذِينَ يُطِيقُونَهُۥ فِدْيَةٌ طَعَامُ مِسْكِينٍۖ فَمَن تَطَوَّعَ خَيْرًا فَهُوَ خَيْرٌ لَّهُۥۚ وَأَن تَصُومُوا۟ خَيْرٌ لَّكُمْۖ إِن كُنتُمْ تَعْلَمُونَ﴾

But those who are not able to fast, obligatory on them is to provide food for a needy person in lieu of that. But whoever does (greater) good seeking pleasure that is better for him. And your fasting is better for you if you understand.[126]

---

[125] Qurʾān, *al-Baqara*, 2:185.
[126] Qurʾān, *al-Baqara*, 2:184.

Q.77. Under what conditions can ransom be paid instead of fasting?

A: If somebody is unable to fast at all for reasons of age-related extreme weakness or a debilitating illness which does not give him the slightest hope of being able to fast all year round (be the days short or long, in harsh or mild or calm weather) in his life, he is allowed to pay ransom instead of fasting. The thought of making *al-qaḍāʾ* or paying ransom for the fast of Ramaḍān based on mild illness is utterly wrong. So is the thought of having acquired all the blessings of the Ramaḍān fast by just paying ransom. One is only allowed to pay ransom when he is absolutely unable to fast.

Q.78. What is the ransom of a Ramaḍān fast?

A: It is to provide an indigent person with two meals per fast. Alternatively, one can give a needy person 2 kg of wheat or 4 kg of barley or some other grains, such as rice, etc. One can also pay its retail market price instead. Ransom per fast is as much as *ṣadaqa al-Fiṭr*[127] per person.

Q.79. If somebody dies before performing some fast that was an obligation or imperative upon him, what is the ruling about making *al-qaḍāʾ* on his behalf?

A: If somebody dies without performing the fast obligated upon him, ransom must be paid, obligatorily, from the money he has left behind (before it is distributed amongst his heirs as inheritance), in the case where he leaves behind a directive will to do so. It is acceptable if his heirs

[127] Obligatory alms given at the end of the month of Ramaḍān and before the prayer of *ʿĪd al-Fiṭr*.

paid from their own money, in the case that he had not left money or a directive will. Ransom per fast is as much as *ṣadaqa al-Fiṭr* per person. ʿAbd Allāh b. ʿUmar ﷺ narrates that the Prophet ﷺ said:

مَنْ مَاتَ وَعَلَيْهِ صِيَامُ شَهْرٍ، فَلْيُطْعَمْ عَنْهُ مَكَانَ كُلِّ يَوْمٍ مِسْكِيْنٌ.

> 'If somebody died after the fast of one month had been obligated upon him, then one needy person must be fed for each day.'[128]

If the deceased did not leave enough money, then we all must seek Allah's forgiveness for him in case the heirs are unable to afford the ransom either. Indeed, Allah ﷻ is Oft-Forgiving and Most Compassionate.

Q.80. If somebody breaks the fast after he has eaten something out of forgetfulness, what is the Shariah ruling in this case?

A: After eating something out of forgetfulness, if a person believes he has broken his fast and eats again on purpose, he is liable to *al-qadāʾ* only and not *al-kaffāra*.

Q.81. Why does eating or drinking by forgetfulness not break the fast?

A: Because the one who fasts does not intend to violate the sanctity of the fast. As a matter of fact, he does not even know at the time that he is keeping fast. Abū Hurayra ﷺ narrates that the Prophet ﷺ said:

مَنْ نَسِيَ وَهُوَ صَائِمٌ فَأَكَلَ أَوْ شَرِبَ فَلْيُتِمَّ صَوْمَهُ. فَإِنَّمَا أَطْعَمَهُ اللهُ وَسَقَاهُ.

[128] Narrated by Ibn Mājah in *al-Sunan*, 2:366 §1757.

> 'Whoever eats or drinks, having forgotten he is fasting, let him complete his fast. For it is only Allah ﷻ who has made him eat and drink.'[129]

In another hadith, Abū Hurayra ؓ narrates that a person came before the Prophet ﷺ and said that he had had some food out of forgetfulness while fasting (meaning to ask what he should do in this case). The holy Prophet ﷺ said,

> 'Allah ﷻ made you eat and drink.'[130]

The majority of imams agree that neither *al-qaḍā'* or atonement is obligated upon the person who has eaten or drunk out of forgetfulness while fasting. He should rather complete his fast (for it has not been nullified). He should consider his state of forgetfulness as a favour of Allah's hospitality. But he must spit it out the very moment he recalls his fast. All that he has taken before he recalls himself is forgiven. A single grain or a single drop passing into the throat after recalling the state of fasting will break the fast.

Q.82. Are we allowed to remind a person of his fast if we find him eating or drinking something?

A: In this case it is imperative to remind him of his fast. It is sinful not to. But one should turn his eyes away if the one fasting is very weak and is apparently unable to complete his fast if he does not eat, regardless of his age. For some old people are strong enough to complete their fast, and some who are young are too weak to do so for some reason, for example, some disease or a significant loss of blood in an accident. If somebody is young but too

---

[129] Narrated by Muslim in *al-Ṣaḥīḥ*, 2:809 §1155.

[130] Narrated by Abū Dawūd in *al-Sunan*, 2:307 §2398.

weak to carry on with his fast for the rest of the day, along with fulfilling his other duties including his worshipful service, then it is preferable to let him eat and not remind him of his fast. If somebody is aged but strong enough to complete fast with all other responsibilities, then it is imperative to remind him.

Q.83. If somebody happens to break his fast during Ramaḍān, can he eat or drink during the rest of the day?

A: If a healthy person happens to break his fast during the holy month of Ramaḍān, then he must not eat or drink anything until dusk as a mark of respect for Ramaḍān. The ruling is the same for a traveller if he reaches home during daytime in Ramaḍān; a pre-pubescent who becomes pubescent; a woman who completes her monthly bleeding circle or her post-natal bleeding ends; or one who is insane regains sanity. Each must observe respect for Ramaḍān and avoid eating or drinking anything at all till dusk.

Q.84. Is a traveller allowed to fast?

A: If the travel involves enough distance to obligate shortening the prayer, then the traveller is allowed to miss his fast. It is still best to fast if the travel does not involve hard circumstances. In our times, trains, cars, planes and other means of transport have made travel quite comfortable and trouble-free. So, whoever can fast without trouble, it is best that he do so. Allah ﷻ states in the Qur᾿ān:

(أَيَّامًا مَّعْدُودَاتٍ ۚ فَمَن كَانَ مِنكُم مَّرِيضًا أَوْ عَلَىٰ سَفَرٍ
فَعِدَّةٌ مِّنْ أَيَّامٍ أُخَرَ ۚ وَعَلَى ٱلَّذِينَ يُطِيقُونَهُۥ فِدْيَةٌ طَعَامُ

$$مِسْكِينٍ فَمَن تَطَوَّعَ خَيْرًا فَهُوَ خَيْرٌ لَّهُ وَأَن تَصُومُواْ خَيْرٌ لَّكُمْ إِن كُنتُمْ تَعْلَمُونَ$$

(These are) a fixed number of days. So, whoever amongst you is ill or on a journey, then he shall complete fasting for the fixed number by (fasting on) other days. But those who are not able to fast, obligatory on them is it to provide food for a needy person in lieu of that. But whoever does (greater) good seeking pleasure that is better for him. And your fasting is better for you if you understand. [131]

A large majority of the jurists hold that the traveller has an option of keeping or missing the fast equally. This is why some of the Companions 🙏, while travelling with the Prophet 🙏, would keep fast while some others would miss it. None of them would ever blame the other. The following hadith narrated by Ibn ʿAbbās 🙏 explains it:

$$لَا تَعِبْ عَلَى مَنْ صَامَ وَلَا عَلَى مَنْ أَفْطَرَ. قَدْ صَامَ رَسُولُ اللهِ ﷺ$$

$$فِي السَّفَرِ وَأَفْطَرَ.$$

'(While travelling) do not decry either the one who keeps or misses his fast. For the Prophet 🙏 kept his fast sometimes while travelling and missed it sometimes.' [132]

Q.85. IF SOMEBODY REMAINS IN A STATE OF MAJOR RITUAL IMPURITY UNTIL AFTER THE BREAK OF DAWN, WILL HIS FAST BE VALID?

A: According to the majority of jurists, his fast is valid in that case. But it is imperative to take the ritual bath

---

[131] Qurʾān, *al-Baqara*, 2:184.
[132] Narrated by Muslim in *al-Ṣaḥīḥ*, 2:785 §1113.

before sunrise in order to pray Fajr prayer. If he does not, he will be sinful. It is utterly disapproved of to remain in such a state while fasting.

Q.86. What is the ruling about women, whether they are allowed to fast or not, during their menstrual or post-natal bleeding cycles?

A: She is not allowed to fast in either case. She has to miss them for as many days as the bleeding continues. After Ramaḍān, she will have to make *al-qaḍā*ʾ of all the fasts she had to miss. ʿĀʾisha ﵂ was reported to have said that the Prophet ﷺ would direct them to fast after regaining purity.[133]

Q.87. Why do women have to make *al-qaḍā*ʾ for the fasts missed for menstrual or post-natal bleeding, whereas they are excused from making *al-qaḍā*ʾ for the prayer missed for the same reason?

A: It is forbidden for women to fast during their monthly or post-natal bleeding. If a woman does so, the fast will be invalid and *al-qaḍā*ʾ will still be imperative. Islam is a religion of easiness, for it is well-synchronised with natural human dispositions. The Shariah has settled the injunctions and teachings of Islam in a manner so beautiful that it does not leave any individual feeling oppressed or restricted, in the course of their practical application. Muʿādha al-ʿAdawiyya ﵂ said that she asked the Mother of the Believers ʿĀʾisha ﵂ why it was that a woman makes *al-qaḍā*ʾ in case of the fasts missed for

---

[133] Narrated by al-Tirmidhī in *al-Sunan*, 2:145 §787.

monthly periods, but she does not do so in case of prayer. ʿĀʾisha ﷺ said,

> 'We used to have this problem (of menstruation). We would receive directive to make *al-qadā*ʾ for the fasts missed, but not for the prayer.'[134]

This word of ʿĀʾishah ﷺ expresses the fact that the acceptance of the injunctions of the Shariah, both positive and negative without 'all the whys and the wherefores' marks true obedience and adherence.

Looking for an apparent reasoning, we might conclude that making *al-qaḍā*ʾ for prayer missed for menstruation which is about seven days per month on average, although it varies between 3 to 10 days for different women, is a rather difficult task to accomplish. So, the Shariah has sanctioned a concession for women here. Making *al-qaḍā*ʾ for the fasts missed during Ramaḍān, on the other hand, happens only once a year, which makes it only seven fasts a year. This is quite easy and practical, particularly when they do not have to be seriatim. So, the Shariah has taken that into consideration when obligating the *al-qadā'* for fasts and excusing them from that of prayer.

Q.88. If menstrual bleeding stops before the break of dawn, are we allowed to keep fast even before having had the obligatory ritual bath?

A: If bleeding stops before the break of dawn and the time left is only enough for eating pre-dawn meal and the minimum or ritual bath cannot be accommodated, then a woman is allowed to take pre-dawn meal with just ablution. She must intend to fast the following day before

---

[134] Narrated by Muslim in *al-Ṣaḥīḥ*, 1:265 §335.

dawn breaks. But she should not delay performing the ritual bath after dawn has broken.

Q.89. Does it break the fast if a woman starts her menses just before dusk?

A: Yes, it does. If she starts her menses at any time between dawn and dusk, even if it is just a few minutes before dusk it breaks her fast and she will have to make *al-qaḍāʾ* for the fast.

Q.90. What is the ruling of the Shariah regarding the fast of a woman who is pregnant or breast feeding?

A: If a pregnant or breast-feeding woman believes on the basis of an expert doctor's professional opinion that fasting will bring harm to her or to her child,[135] she is allowed to miss the fast. But she will have to make *al-qaḍāʾ* for those fasts later. Allah ﷻ states:

(وَمَن كَانَ مَرِيضًا أَوْ عَلَىٰ سَفَرٍ فَعِدَّةٌ مِّنْ أَيَّامٍ أُخَرَ)

---

[135] Harm means stopping the growth of the child or cause serious illness or she won't be able to produce enough milk to fulfil the child's need. Harm to her means that she will become seriously ill; or she will not be able to carry out her routine household work while there is no possibility of anybody else taking over the work from her; or it is impossible for her to take days off her work and the debility will affect her seriously if she carries on attending her work. This is the situation that allows her to miss the fast of Ramaḍān. Otherwise, the fast of Ramaḍān is too precious to be missed just for pregnancy or breastfeeding. Losing the blessings of Ramaḍān is damage beyond repair.

> *And he who is ill or on a journey should complete the count by (fasting on equal number of) other days.*[136]

Q.91. Can a cook or chef or a woman working in the kitchen taste what they cook while fasting?

A: They can do so provided that the substance being tasted does not reach their throat. It is same for all Ramaḍān, imperative and optional fasts. Ibn ʿAbbās ﵄ said:

لَا بَأْسَ أَنْ يَتَطَعَّمَ الْقِدْرَ أَوِ الشَّيْءَ.

> 'It does not bring any harm to taste the pot or something.'[137]

Q.92. What does the word tasting signify in this regard?

A: 'To taste' something means to place it on the front part of the tongue in order to gauge the taste, so as to know if everything is all right or if it needs something more and then spit it out before it moves towards the throat. The generally understood process of tasting something, which allows eating some of it for tasting it, is not meant here because it will break the fast and obligate *al-qaḍāʾ* as well as atonement if it qualifies for that such as the fast in Ramaḍān.

---

[136] Qurʾān, *al-Baqara*, 2:185.

[137] Narrated by al-Bukhārī in *al-Ṣaḥīḥ*, 2:618 §1828.

Q.93. ARE WE ALLOWED TO WEAR LIPSTICK OR TO APPLY PETROLEUM JELLY TO THE LIPS?

A: Yes, we are allowed to wear them provided that their substance does not reach the throat.

Q.94. ARE WE ALLOWED TO WEAR KOHL WHILE FASTING?w

A: Yes, we are. Anas ؓ narrates that a person who had had some problem with his eyes appeared in the holy presence of the Holy Prophet ﷺ and asked if he could wear kohl. The Prophet ﷺ told him that he could (wear kohl while fasting).[138]

Q.95. WHAT IS THE RULING ABOUT GARGLING AND INHALING WATER UP THE NOSTRILS WHILE FASTING?

A: One is allowed to gargle and inhale water up the nostrils while fasting. But one cannot overdo so. Exaggerating them while fasting, is strongly disapproved although we are meant to exaggerate them if not fasting. The Holy Prophet ﷺ said:

أَسْبِغِ الْوُضُوءَ وَخَلِّلْ بَيْنَ الْأَصَابِعِ، وَبَالِغْ فِي الإِسْتِنْشَاقِ إِلاَّ أَنْ تَكُونَ صَائِمًا.

> 'Perform your ablution fully. Interlace your fingers and exaggerate the inhalation of water up the nostrils unless you are fasting.'[139]

Exaggerating a gargle means to gargle with a gurgle, many times provoking the feeling that the water has gone down the throat. Exaggerating in inhaling water up the

---

[138] Narrated by al-Tirmidhī in *al-Sunan*, 2:97 §726.
[139] Narrated by al-Tirmidhī in *al-Sunan*, 3:155 §788.

nostrils means to inhale water up to the uppermost part of the bridge of the nose, many times so that the water reaches the actual bone on top of it.

Let us not forget here that if water unintentionally reaches the throat, while exaggerating either gargling or inhaling water up the nostrils, it will break the fast and obligate *al-qadā*ʾ unless it happens when the one fasting does not recall he is fasting.

Q.96. Are we allowed to clean our teeth with the teeth cleaning twig or tooth paste?

A: Yes, we are. We are allowed to clean our teeth with the teeth cleaning twig (*al-miswāk*). It is Sunna to use *al-miswāk*, whether wet or dry. We are also allowed to use tooth paste, provided that we can make sure that neither its particles nor its taste reaches the throat. But the use of tood paste or tooth powder is not recommended.

Q.97. Does bleeding of the gums break the fast?

A: If the blood overwhelms the saliva and reaches into the throat, it will break the fast, regardless of whether it reaches the throat by itself or the person swallows it. This will obligate *al-qaḍā*ʾ, but not atonement. If the saliva overwhelms the blood, the fast is not broken.

Q.98. Does vomiting break the fast?

A: Vomit does not nullify the fast, if it is less than a mouthful[140] (like spew). If somebody makes himself vomit, for example emetically, he breaks his fast unless

[140] 'A mouthful of vomit' means as much or with such force that the person vomiting just cannot keep his mouth closed without some exertion.

the vomit is less than a mouthful. Abū Hurayra 🙏 narrates that the Prophet ﷺ said:

مَنْ ذَرَعَهُ الْقَيْءُ فَلَيْسَ عَلَيْهِ قَضَاءٌ، وَمِنِ اسْتَقَاءَ عَمَداً فَلْيَقْضِ.

'If (a want to) vomit overwhelms somebody (hence he cannot control it) while he is fasting he does not need to make al-qaḍā' (the fast is intact). If somebody makes himself vomit purposefully, he must expiate for it.'[141]

Q.99. DOES HAVING AN INJECTION OR BEING ON A DRIP NULLIFY THE FAST?

A: Yes, the use of a drip or injection or any other thing that can be considered dietary or medicinal and exerts an influence upon the stomach or brain, will nullify the fast. If somebody is quite seriously ill he already enjoys the approval, rather the recommendation, of missing the fast from the Shariah. In some cases, he must nullify his fast and use diet and medicine as directed by a medical expert. If the condition seems to be fatal, he will be forbidden to fast and be deemed sinful if he does.

Q.100. ARE THOSE WHO ARE ASTHMATIC ALLOWED TO USE AN INHALER WHILE FASTING?

A: An inhaler does not contain oxygen only, it also contains some medicine which exerts its medical effect on the heart and stomach. This is why one must avoid it. If the one fasting cannot do without it and his breathing conditions are severe, he should miss his fast. If his health condition is such that there is no gleam of hope that he will ever be able to fast in his life, he should pay ransom for his fasts. The amount of ransom per fast is as much as

---

[141] Narrated by al-Tirmidhī in al-Sunan, 2:90 §720.

ṣadaqa al-Fiṭr per person (2 kg of wheat or wheat-flour or its price) payable to an indigent or needy person, everyday for that particular day or in one instance for the whole month, given to different people for different fasts or to only one person for all of them.

Q.101. Is it permissible to give blood to somebody while fasting?

A: The recipient of the blood transfusion must not keep fast. The donor should be careful about his own health and fast. Giving blood does not nullify the fast, but it may cause the donor some weakness. So, the donor should only do so if he is satisfied that he will not only be able to keep his fast, but he will also not suffer from debility. If somebody's life is in danger (and there is no other source of blood for that person), then he must carry out the obligation of saving a human life as well as keeping his fast intact, even if he has to face some trouble from the consequent weakness till dusk.

Q.102. Does inhaling smoke, dust, the fragrance of a perfume or incense fumes (without one's intention and action) nullify the fast?

A: No, it does not nullify the fast. But inhaling it on purpose and feeling the particles in the throat will break the fast. So much so that if someone burns the incense for somebody else and smells it; then recalls he is fasting but still allows the particles to reach the throat, he has nullified his fast. The jurists have differentiated between penetration of smoke, dust, incense-fumes or particles of fragrance to the throat and inhaling them purposefully. The latter is the action, which could have been avoided by the one fasting. This is further supported by the word of the author of *al-Nihāya,* which says that it does not nullify the fast if somehow a fly happens to reach the stomach. For nothing contrary to the fast, such as taking something in deliberately, has been found.

5. *Al-Iʿtikāf* (Spiritual Retreat)

Q.103. What does *al-iʿtikāf* mean?

A: *Al-Iʿtikāf* is an Arabic word which literally means 'to seclude or isolate oneself, to restrain oneself, to withdraw or retire, to devote or adhere to somebody, to be engaged with somebody in a way that even one's eyes do not turn away from him'.[142]

As a term of the Shariah, it means 'to stay in a mosque for a specific span of time, while detached from all worldly relations, with the intention of worshipful service so as to revive one's relation of worshipful service to Allah ﷻ, with the help of total seclusion'.

Q.104. How important is it to perform spiritual retreat?

A: A number of hadiths have been reported that assert the importance of spiritual retreat. We mention some of them below:

1. ʿAbd Allāh b. ʿAbbās ﷠ narrates that Allah's Messenger ﷺ said about *al-muʿtakif*,[143]

> 'He avoids sins and is granted his rewards generously like a practical worker of righteous deeds.'[144]

---

[142] Ibn Manẓūr, *Lisān al-ʿArab*, 9:255.

[143] Somebody who performs *al-iʿtikāf* is called *al-muʿtakif*.

[144] Narrated by Ibn Mājah in *al-Sunan*, 2:376 §1781.

2. According to another hadith narrated by ʿAbd Allāh b. ʿAbbās ⬤, the holy Prophet ⬤ said:

مَنِ اعْتَكَفَ يَوْمًا ابْتِغَاءَ وَجْهِ اللهِ ﷾ ، جَعَلَ اللهُ بَيْنَهُ وَبَيْنَ النَّارِ ثَلَاثَ خَنَادِقَ، كُلُّ خَنْدَقٍ أَبْعَدُ مِمَّا بَيْنَ الْخَافِقَيْنِ.

'Whoever performs a one day seclution for the sake of Allah's good pleasure, Allah ﷾ will make three trenches between him and Hell; each trench is longer than the distance between the East and the West.'[145]

3. Imām ʿAlī Zayn al-ʿĀbidīn b. Ḥusayn narrates that his father Imām Ḥusayn ⬤ told him that the Prophet ⬤ had said:

مَنِ اعْتَكَفَ عَشْرًا فِي رَمَضَانَ، كَانَ كَحَجَّتَيْنِ وَعُمْرَتَيْنِ.

'Whoever performs spiritual retreat for ten days in Ramaḍān, its reward is like that of two pilgrimages and two minor pilgrimages.'[146]

Q.105. DURING WHAT DAYS OF RAMAḌĀN IS IT AL-MASNŪN TO PERFORM SPIRITUAL RETREAT?

A: It is Sunna to perform spiritual retreat during the last ten days of Ramaḍān. ʿAbd Allāh b. ʿUmar ⬤ said:

أَنَّ رَسُولَ اللهِ ﷺ كَانَ يَعْتَكِفُ الْعَشْرَ الْأَوَاخِرَ مِنْ رَمَضَانَ.

'The holy Prophet ⬤ used to perform spiritual retreat during the last ten days of Ramaḍān.'[147]

---

[145] Narrated by al-Ṭabarānī in *al-Muʿjam al-Awsaṭ*, 7:221 §7326; al-Bayhaqī in *Shuʿab al-Īmān*, 3:425 §3965; and al-Haythamī in *Mawārid al-Ẓamʾān*, 8:192.

[146] Narrated by al-Bayhaqī in *Shuʿab al-Īmān*, 3:425 §3966.

[147] Narrated by Ibn Mājah in *al-Sunan*, 2:373 §1773.

Q.106. According to the Shariah, when does seclusion founded on the Prophetic practice commence and when does it end?

A: According to the Shariah, it commences just before dusk on the 20th of Ramaḍān and ends just after the moon sighting of Shawwāl, which could be on the 29th or 30th of Ramaḍān.

Q.107. What are the conditions for a person to perform spiritual retreat?

A: The following are the prerequisites of spiritual retreat:

- Islam (the performer's being Muslim)
- Intention of spiritual retreat
- Ritual purity (being free of menstrual or post-natal bleeding or major ritual impurity)
- Sanity
- Performing it in a mosque
- Fasting (for the imperative spiritual retreat)

Q.108. How many types of spiritual retreat are there?

A: There are three types of spiritual retreat:

- Imperative—such as the one based on a vow (*al-wājib*)
- Founded on the Prophetic practice (*al-masnūn*)
- Optional (*al-nafl*)

Q.109. What is emphatically enjoined Sunna of spiritual retreat?

A: The spiritual retreat during the last ten days of Ramaḍān is known as *al-sunna al-muʾakkada ʿalā al-kifāya*. This means that if all of the people in a certain locality omit it, every person amongst them will be blamed. However, if one of them performs it, none will be blamed on the Day of Judgement. More plainly, this is not a responsibility upon every individual in a locality. It is rather a collective responsibility, which is lifted from all the people in a locality if some of them perform it. ʿAbd Allāh b. ʿUmar ﷺ narrates that the Prophet ﷺ used to perform spiritual retreat for the last ten days of Ramaḍān.[148]

Q.110. What is optional spiritual retreat?

A: Any spiritual retreat other than imperative or founded on the Prophetic practice, is called optional spiritual retreat. One of the things different about this one is that it does not require fasting or a minimum time-span or specific timing, as essential elements. So, if somebody enters a mosque at any time of the day, for any length of time, he can intend seclusion. He will be granted the reward of performing seclusion for as long as he remains in the mosque in that instance. All he needs to do is to intend in his heart and say with his tongue 'I intend to perform the Sunna of spiritual retreat for the sake of Allah'.

Q.111. What is necessary/vow spiritual retreat?

A: If somebody made a vow that he would observe a three-day spiritual retreat for Allah's sake if such and such matter were resolved. This obligates spiritual retreat upon him and he has to perform it once that matter is resolved. This is necessary seclusion and requires intention and fasting as an essential part, it cannot be

---

[148] Ibid.

performed without being accompanied by intention and fasting.

Q.112. What is the minimum time span for necessary spiritual retreat?

A: Since fasting is a condition for necessary spiritual retreat , it cannot be for less than 24 hours.

Q.113. What deeds should *al-muʿtakif* adopt?

A: *Al-Muʿtakif* must include the following deeds in his routine during spiritual retreat:

- Recitation of the Qurʾān
- To keep the tongue busy with seeking blessings for and sending salutations to the Prophet ﷺ
- To study or teach religious sciences
- Give good advice and admonition
- Standing up in optional worshipful service of Allah, offering prayer
- Busying oneself with the remembrance of Allah.

Q.114. What is the legal status of collective spiritual retreat?

A: The renowned jurist Ibn Rushd holds that the difference of opinion about its being valid or invalid is based on the difference of opinion about the exact significance of spiritual retreat. He writes:

فَمَنْ فَهِمَ مِنَ الْإِعْتِكَافِ حَبْسَ النَّفْسِ عَلَى الْأَفْعَالِ الْـمُخْتَصَّةِ بِالْـمَسَاجِدِ، قَالَ: لاَ يَجُوْزُ لِلْمُعْتَكِفِ إِلَّا الصَّلَاةُ وَالْقِرَاءَةُ، وَمَنْ

فَهِمَ مِنْهُ حَبْسَ النَّفْسِ عَلَى الْقُرُبِ الْأُخْرُوِيَّةِ كُلِّهَا أَجَازَ لَهُ غَيْرَ ذَلِكَ.

> Those who understand that spiritual retreat holds the meaning of confining oneself to the deeds specific to a mosque, have only allowed for *al-muʿtakif* to perform prayer and recitation. Those, on the other hand, who believe that it means to confine oneself to the acquisition of divine proximity in the hereafter, rather than some specific deeds, have allowed for him more than that.[149]

The difference between individual and collective matters

Individual acts of worship such as reciting the Qurʾān, prayer, remembrance of Allah are permissible for *al-muʿtakif* unanimously and without any form of difference. Concerning the acts of worship which require gathering together with others or take a collective form, the jurists have not only generally allowed them like those of an individual nature but also declared them necessary in certain circumstances. Such collective acts of worship include enjoining good, prohibiting evil, responding to greetings, issuing religious verdicts, guiding people to the truth and other deeds of the sort. Although it is best not to involve too much time with them (when done collectively).

But the scholars do differ in their opinion about the matters that take a lot of time, such as getting involved with studying, teaching and discussing religious matters and the study of the Qurʾān and the hadith. Hanafite and

---

[149] Ibn Rushd, *Bidāya al-Mujtahid*, 1:312.

Shafiite scholars, however, declare them lawful for *al-muᶜtakif*.[150]

Collective Matters that can be dealt with by *al-muᶜtakif*

Al-muᶜtakif can attend many matters. We mention here some of them:

Al-Qaḍā᾽

If a person is a judge or is capable of passing judgement in matters of dispute amongst people, he must decide the matter brought to him while still *al-muᶜtakif*, particularly when the decisive evidence is also fully presented before him. Imām al-Shāfiᶜī writes in *al-Umm* (2:105):

وَلاَ بَأْسَ أَنْ يَقْضِيَ وَإِنْ كَانَتْ عِنْدَهُ شَهَادَةٌ، فَدُعِيَ إِلَيْهَا فَإِنَّهُ يَلْزَمُهُ أَنْ يُجِيبَ.

> Passing judgement in a matter does not produce any harm (for *al-muᶜtakif* regarding his spiritual retreat). If he is requested to attend with decisive witness made available to him, he must respond.

Learning and teaching

Mother of the Believers ᶜĀ᾽isha ﵂ narrates:

وَكَانَ يُخْرِجُ رَأْسَهُ ﷺ إِلَيَّ وَهُوَ مُعْتَكِفٌ، فَأَغْسِلُهُ وَأَنَا حَائِضٌ.

> He ﷺ would move his head out of the mosque towards me while he was *al-muᶜtakif* and I would wash it while I was menstruating.[151]

Al-Khattābī comments on this hadith:

---

[150] Ibn al-Hammām, *Fatḥ al-Qadīr*, 2:396; al-Shāfiᶜī, *al-Umm*, 2:105; al-Nawawī, *al-Majmūᶜ*, 6:528; al-Māwardī, *al-Iqnāᶜ*, 1:229; *al-Fatāwā al-Hindiyya*, 1:212.

[151] Narrated by al-Bukhārī in *al-Ṣaḥīḥ*, 1:115 §295.

فَإِنَّ الْإِشْتِغَالَ بِالْعِلْمِ وَكِتَابَتِهِ أَهَمُّ مِنْ تَسْرِيْحِ الشَّعْرِ.

> Busying oneself with the acquisition of knowledge and (saving it by) writing it, is definitely more important than combing one's hair.[152]

So, it is best to involve oneself with learning and teaching, which also enables us to act upon the universal injunction of Islam that our beloved Prophet ﷺ received in the very first divine revelation to him and was heavily emphasised in both the Qurʾān and hadith. Imām al-Shāfiʿī writes in *al-Umm* (2:105):

وَلاَ بَأْسَ أَنْ يَشْتَرِيَ وَيَبِيعَ وَيَخِيطَ وَيُجَالِسَ الْعُلَمَاءِ وَيَتَحَدَّث بِمَا أَحَبَّ مَا لَمْ يَكُنْ إِثْمًا.

> It does not matter (for *al-muʿtakif*) to undertake commercial transactions (if needed), to sew (if needed), to take company with scholars and to talk what he likes as long as it does not amount to sin.

If *al-muʿtakif* can deal with necessary commercial transactions when he needs to for his life and that of his dependents; can sew his clothes if he needs to, the involvement with acquiring knowledge which brings him close to Allah ﷻ, definitely possesses far greater importance. Adding to that, to gain knowledge is an activity that has enjoyed definite preference with the practice of our beloved Prophet ﷺ. Once when there were two sessions being convened in the Prophetic mosque, one for the remembrance of Allah and the other for spreading knowledge, he ﷺ attended the latter.

---

[152] Zayn al-Dīn al-ʿIrāqī, *Ṭarḥ al-Tathrīb fī Sharḥ al-Taqrīb*, 4:175.

BUYING AND SELLING IF NECESSARY

One is also allowed to buy or sell during spiritual retreat, provided that the merchandise is not inside the mosque and the matter does not exceed offer-and-acceptance. This condition is based upon the sanctity of the mosque, which must not be transgressed and not a requirement of spiritual retreat. In this regard, we find Imam al-Shāfiʿī writes in *al-Umm* (2:105):

> It does not matter if a *muʿtakif* undertakes commercial transactions (if needed), to sew (if needed), to take company with scholars and to talk what he likes as long as it does not amount to sin.[153]

Imam al-Kāsānī also quotes the word of ʿAlī ؓ as follows:

وَرُوِيَ عَنْ عَلِيٍّ ؓ أَنَّهُ قَالَ لِابْنِ أَخِيهِ جَعْفَرٍ: هَلاَّ اشْتَرَيْتَ خَادِمًا؟ قَالَ: كُنْتُ مُعْتَكِفًا. قَالَ: وَمَاذَا عَلَيْكَ لَوِ اشْتَرَيْتَ؟ —

أَشَارَ إِلَى جَوَازِ الشِّرَاءِ فِي الْـمَسْجِدِ.

> It has been reported about ʿAlī ؓ that he said to his nephew Jaʿfar ؓ, 'Why did you not buy a servant?' He said he was in seclusion (*al-iʿtikāf*). ʿAlī ؓ said, 'What would have happened if you had bought one?' This indicates the permission of buying inside the mosque (during *iʿtikāf*).[154]

The same is the case with other commercial dealings which do not take time. They are allowed because they resemble the response to a greeting or a sneeze.

---

[153] Also narrated by al-Kāsānī in *Badāʾiʿ al-Ṣanāʾiʿ*, 2:117; and al-Nawawī in *al-Majmūʿ*, 6:533.

[154] Al-Kāsānī, *Badāʾiʿ al-Ṣanāʾiʿ*, 2:117.

Meeting family and conversing with them

If one comes for *al-iʿtikāf* after almost a whole year, it does not mean that he detaches himself from all matters related to others, or those resembling busying oneself with creation. The impressions from the biography of the holy Prophet ﷺ prove quite contrary to this. We find instances of meeting the Companions ؓ, advising them when needed and meeting with family members. ʿĀʾishah ؓ narrates:

وَكَانَ يُخْرِجُ رَأْسَهُ ﷺ إِلَيَّ وَهُوَ مُعْتَكِفٌ، فَأَغْسِلُهُ وَأَنَا حَائِضٌ.

> 'He ﷺ would move his head out of the mosque towards me while he was *al-muʿtakif* and I would wash it, while I was menstruating.'[155]

We also find the hadith of the Mother of the Believers Ṣafiyya ؓ which explains what has been narrated by ʿAli b. Ḥusayn ؓ. He said that the Prophet ﷺ was in the mosque. His wife was also with him. When she was about to leave after the completion of their conversation, the Prophet ﷺ told her to wait and that he would also come with her (to walk her home) because her chamber was (at some distance) at the house of Usāma ؓ. When they came out of the mosque, they came across two Medinan Helper Companions. Both of them went past when they saw the Prophet ﷺ. The holy Prophet ﷺ called them both and said:

تَعَالَيَا! إِنَّهَا صَفِيَّةُ بِنْتُ حُيَيٍّ.

> 'Come here! This is (your mother) Ṣafiyya bint Ḥuyayy.'

They said, 'Glorified is Allah, O Allah's Messenger! (How on earth can we think anything wrong of you?)'

---

[155] Narrated by al-Bukhārī in *al-Ṣaḥīḥ*, 1:115 §295.

Allah's Messenger ﷺ responded, 'Satan runs like blood in a human's body. I feared lest he should whisper doubts in your heart.'[156]

Enjoining good and prohibiting evil

The above mentioned hadith asserts the permissibility of talking to family members. At the same time, it confirms permission to go out of the mosque if and as much as needed. It also explains that we are allowed to carry out enjoining the good and prohibiting the evil while performing spiritual retreat. The Prophet ﷺ noticed it was possible for some evil thought to occupy their minds. Acting upon his instinct and caring for their faith, the Prophet ﷺ prevented such an occurrence.[157] Also the Prophet ﷺ was outside his place of spiritual retreat at that moment. With this in mind, how can we declare enjoining good and prohibiting evil, which is a practice of collective nature, contrary to spiritual retreat?

Limited permission of matters related to marriage

Marriage helps lay the foundations of sociability and togetherness in a society, as well as strengthening them. Although *al-muʿtakif* is confined to a corner of a mosque in isolation from all such matters, the respected leading scholars have not seen it fit to forbid him from undertaking the marriage contract, attending a *nikāḥ* ceremony, inviting somebody else to attend it or congratulating the bridegroom, provided that all this

---

[156] Narrated by al-Bukhārī in *al-Ṣaḥīḥ*, 2:716 §1933.

[157] Those two people could have fallen victim to Satan's whispers if they did not know who the woman with the Prophet ﷺ was. If Satan had been able to succeed in instilling wrong thoughts about the Prophet ﷺ into their minds they would become disbelievers straight away.

happens inside the mosque where he is performing spiritual retreat. They have also considered lawful the act of offering condolences and reconciling opponents. This is the view of the majority of jurists.

وَلاَ بَأْسَ لِلْمُعْتَكِفِ أَنْ يَبِيْعَ وَيَشْتَرِيَ وَيَتَزَوَّجَ وَيُرَاجِعَ وَيَلْبَسَ وَيَتَطَيَّبَ وَيَدَّهِنَ، وَيَأْكُلَ وَيَشْرَبَ بَعْدَ غُرُوْبِ الشَّمْسِ إِلَى طُلُوْعِ الْفَجْرِ، وَيَتَحَدَّثَ مَا بَدَا لَهُ بَعْدَ أَنْ لاَ يَكُوْنَ مَأْثَمًا وَيَنَامُ فِي الْـمَسْجِدِ.

> It does not harm *al-muʿtakif* if he sells or buys or gets married or revises (his lessons, for example) or gets changed or wears perfume or embrocate oil or eats, drinks, talks what he likes if it is not a sin from dusk to dawn (all night from *al-Maghrib* to *al-Fajr*). He can also sleep in the mosque.[158]

Inquiring after a sick person

Like many other things, visiting a sick person to inquire after his health has also been substantiated by the Prophet's biography. ʿĀʾishah ﷺ says:

كَانَ النَّبِيُّ ﷺ يَمُرُّ بِالْـمَرِيْضِ وَهُوَ مُعْتَكِفٌ، فَيَمُرُّ كَمَا هُوَ وَلَا يُعَرِّجُ يَسْأَلُ عَنْهُ.

> 'The holy Prophet ﷺ would inquire after a sick person while passing by (and without having stopped), if he was *al-muʿtakif* (and happened to go out of mosque for his need).'[159]

---

[158] Al-Kāsānī, *Badāʾiʿ al-Ṣānāʾiʿ*, 2:117; al-Nawawī, *al-Majmūʿ*, 6:533.

[159] Narrated by Abū Dawūd in *al-Sunan*, 2:333 §2472.

Imam al-Tirmidhī says, as he deduces the permission of inquiring after a sick person:

قَالَتْ: إِنْ كَانَ النَّبِيُّ ﷺ يَعُودُ الْـمَرِيْضَ وَهُوَ مُعْتَكِفٌ.

> ʿĀʾisha ﷺ said that 'the Prophet ﷺ would inquire after the sick person's health during spiritual retreat.'[160]

Objectives of spiritual retreat in the contemporary world

There is no doubt that the main purpose of spiritual retreat is to mend the ways of the lower self, to get rid of evil and to acquire seclusion. Equally notable is the fact that an action cannot produce fruits and stability unless it is based upon a solid foundation, which can only be made available through the means of proper knowledge. This is why all the jurists have unanimously declared the practice of learning and teaching during spiritual retreat, lawful despite the fact that it is a collective activity. The truth of the matter is that spiritual austerity and religious-ecstatic endeavor, cannot lead to any destination without knowledge. The holy Prophet ﷺ said:

فَقِيْهٌ وَاحِدٌ أَشَدُّ عَلَى الشَّيْطَانِ مِنْ أَلْفِ عَابِدٍ.

> 'One jurist is stronger than one thousand (ignorant) worshipful servants against Satan.'[161]

Our problem

Our parents are Muslims. So, we do not value Islam because of the fact that we have inherited it and have not exerted any struggle to search for it. As a direct result, a considerable number of Muslims do not even know *al-*

---

[160] Ibid.

[161] Narrated by Abū Dawūd in *al-Sunan*, 1:181 #222.

shahāda; or what it means if they have learnt it; or what it requires if they have learnt the translation.

Reciting the Qurʾān has been considered the best form of worship, which is amongst the most basic works of spiritual retreat. Unfortunately, the vast majority in countries like ours can't recite it without mistakes. In these circumstances, over-insisting on certain private practices and spending ten days and nights fully confined to invoking some specific prayers, fails the actual purpose of spiritual retreat.

In the light of present-day circumstances, we firmly believe that matters related to individual training and social reformations are far more important than the bare invocation of certain prayers. When society as a whole falls victim to complete wickedness and misguidance, many rulings change. ʿUmar b. ʿAbd al-ʿAzīz says:

إِنَّ اللهَ تَبَارَكَ وَتَعَالَى لَا يُعَذِّبُ الْعَامَّةَ بِذَنْبِ الْخَاصَّةِ، وَلَكِنْ إِذَا عُمِلَ الْمُنْكَرُ جِهَارًا اسْتَحَقُّوا الْعُقُوبَةَ كُلُّهُمْ.

'Allah ﷻ does not punish a people for the sins of particular persons, except that the practice of evil and wickedness is openly adopted. Then all of them deserve divine wrath, indiscriminately.'[162]

Jabir ؓ narrates that the Prophet ﷺ said, 'Allah ﷻ revealed to Jibrīl to destroy such and such a town including its inhabitants.' Jibrīl said, 'O my Lord! There is a person amongst them who has never disobeyed you, (even for the time of) a blink of an eye (do you allow me to spare him?).' Allah responded:

---

[162] Narrated by Mālik in *al-Muwaṭṭā*, 2:991 §23.

أَقْلِبْهَا عَلَيْهِمْ، فَإِنَّ وَجْهَهُ لَمْ يَتَمَعَّرْ فِيَّ سَاعَةً قَطُّ.

> Turn it over upon them (and do not spare him either) because he never frowned for My sake in the face of evil. Not even once![163]

This hadith expressly warns those worshipful servants who are immersed in their own worshipful practices, with an utter lack of concern for others and their correction. This obligation of *al-daʿwa* can only be carried out properly by those whose acts of worshipful service are not confined to their private invocations and prayers, but also include the Prophetic work for the *al-daʿwa* and betterment of the conditions of the *Umma*. Such people do make time especially for that. The above discussion explains the commendability of actions that concern our welfare and correction, as well as that of others. This includes actions such as learning and teaching the Qurʾān, self-purification and others of that category. Such actions are more than just permissible during spiritual retreat, so asserts the preponderant juristic opinion.

To observe long silence during spiritual retreat

Silence is a prelude to the acquisition of wisdom and is the most powerful and well-tested source for protecting our tongue. The teachings of the Qurʾān and hadith value it a great deal. However, taking silence to such an extreme that you are unable to communicate essential things is forbidden.

A hadith, according to which a woman appeared to the Prophet ﷺ and asked if she was allowed to observe the fast along with complete silence on Fridays. To which the Prophet ﷺ replied:

---

[163] Narrated by al-Bayhaqī in *Shuʿab al-Īmān*, 6:97 §7595; and al-Ṭabarānī in *al-Muʿjam al-Awsaṭ*, 7:366 §7661.

لَا تَصُمْ يَوْمَ الْـجُمُعَةِ إِلَّا فِي أَيَّامٍ هُوَ أَحَدُهَا أَوْ فِي شَهْرٍ، وَأَمَّا أَنْ لَا تُكَلِّمَ أَحَدًا، فَلَعَمْرِي! لَأَنْ تَكَلَّمَ بِمَعْرُوْفٍ وَتَنْهَى عَنْ مُنْكَرٍ خَيْرٌ مِنْ أَنْ تَسْكُتَ.

'Do not fast on Fridays (on their own) unless it is one of the days you fast or the month you fast. As for the speech, enjoining good and prohibiting evil is most definitely far better than keeping quiet.'[164]

Examples of collective spiritual retreat

It is clear from the above discussion, that there has been a difference of opinion as to the permissibility or disapproval of collective spiritual retreat. In view of the present conditions of the *Umma*, however, we also find some examples of its performance. Many amongst those who thought it to be invalid under the caption of innovation (*al-bidᶜa*), have started to practice it. The difference between foreseeing circumstances with the heavenly gift of sagacity and the inability to do so has always been present. A righteous person with ranks of Allah's proximity has this radiance of perception to help him with judgement, while those bereft of such light are only able to see reality in due course.

Spiritual retreat in the two sanctuaries of Mecca and Medina

In our times, the largest gathering of spiritual retreat in the world occurs in Mecca and Medina. These sacred places welcome a great number of pilgrims, whose number grows above three figures. In Ramaḍān they earn the prosperity of performing spiritual retreat there.

---

[164] Narrated by Aḥmad b. Ḥanbal in *al-Musnad*, 5:224 §22004; and al-Ṭabarānī in *al-Muᶜjam al-Awsaṭ*, 7:336 §7661.

Although they only allocate specific places and do not set up tents or sheets, it is full of sessions for learning the Qur'ān and hadith. The sessions of *tajwīd al-Qur'ān* (the science of reciting the Qur'ān like the Prophet ﷺ did) and fiqh are also everyday occurrences. The people in spiritual retreat in Mecca also perform circumambulation around the *ka'ba*, something which cannot be done alone. It really is a state of seclusion in the midst of a crowd.

Spiritual retreat under the aegis of Minhaj-ul-Quran

Minhaj-ul-Quran International (MQI) is an organization to promote peace, love and harmony between the religions of the world. Its founding leader, his eminence Shaykh-ul-Islam Professor Dr Muhammad Tahir-ul-Qadri, has withdrawn from the odds of prevalent norms and given the *Umma* a new, thoughtful and vigilant mind. One of its eminent features is its ability to knock at the doors of people's hearts. In that it also follows in the footsteps of the Prophet ﷺ, as he executed his four basic duties as a Prophet, namely reciting the Qur'ān, purifying souls, teaching the Book and equipping others with wisdom, thus defending all the fronts necessary to attend to in our times. It has also achieved a great degree of success in cleaning the rust off souls and cleansing hearts. One of the prominent features of Minhaj-ul-Quran in this regard, is the unconventional event of yearly spiritual retreat. The spiritual retreat (founded on the Prophetic practice) of the last ten days of Ramaḍān, has long been 'spiritual retreat for proper spiritual and moral training' in the sagacious mind of the patron-in-chief of MQI, which he has repeatedly mentioned. He would retreat into his *al-i'tikāf* every year but the practical implications started to assert themselves in 1990, when he had a company of 50 people to join him in spiritual retreat at the MQI central secretariat mosque. The following year in 1991, the number increased and found the mosque too small to accommodate them all. In 1992, when Jāmiʿ al-Minhāj Mosque in Baghdad Town Lahore was declared as the regular place for the annual collective spiritual retreat, the number of participants was 1,500. Today, with the grace of Allah ﷻ, this number has grown to 25,000.[165] For women to join the spiritual retreat, the building of the hostels of the Minhaj Girls' College, near the mosque, has been brought to use. More than 25,000 people, men and women, join this spiritual retreat to purify their inner being and enhance the sweetness of the academic taste.

As mentioned above, this spiritual retreat includes a spiritual and religious training programme, which covers the circles of remembrance of Allah, sending of greetings and salutations to the holy Prophet ﷺ, fiqh sessions and also lessons from the Qurʾān and hadith. Most importantly, the lectures of the revivalist of the present century, his eminence Shaykh-ul-Islam Professor Dr Muhammad Tahir-ul-Qadri, on academic, thought-provoking and spiritual topics, are a perfect source for their intellectual and spiritual enlightenment and pave the way for their self-purification and the cleansing of their hearts. It would not be an exaggeration to say that MQI presents the true concept and accurate practical format of spiritual retreat, founded on the Prophetic practice as required in our time.

Q.115. What are the merits and fruits of collective spiritual retreat?

A: The following are the merits and the fruits of spiritual retreat.

---

[165] It was in 2009. The number of the participants 'in total' has grown to more than 40,000.

• In collective spiritual retreat, a set timetable is observed which allows the participants to perform five-times prayers, pre-dawn optional prayer (*al-tahajjud*), sunrise optional prayer (*al-ishrāq*), mid-morning optional prayer (*al-ḍuḥā*), post-dusk optional prayer (*al-awwābīn*), daily invocations and supplications at their appointed time, nashīd-gatherings, to learn Qur'ān and hadith lessons, to attend circles of *fiqh* and tasawwuf and lectures. The fruits also include initiating God-wariness and thoughtfulness of the hereafter, enkindling hearts with the love of Allah and His Messenger ﷺ, removing contemporary academic and spiritual confusions in the light of the Qur'ān, the Sunna and sound reasoning. A private seclusion cannot have such benefits.

• Amongst the extraordinary features of collective spiritual retreat, we enjoy the blessed company of the righteous and scholars. We also enrich ourselves with their blessings and acquire precious information about the teachings of the Qur'ān, the hadith and Islamic law.

• It helps improve invocations, begging Allah's blessing upon the Prophet ﷺ and sending salutations to him, repentance and beseeching Allah's forgiveness, imploring and worshipful service from ritual routine to a true state of heart and soul.

• It imprints the blessings of a whole spiritual environment, its education and its fervour on the heart, soul and mind to help keep them shining forever. An individual spiritual retreat would not be able to provide all this.

Q.116. What does *Layla al-Qadr* mean and amongst which nights should it be searched?

A: It is a night amongst odd nights, during the last ten days of Ramaḍān. This night is highly respected and carries a great deal of blessings. The Qur'ān has declared it as greater than one thousand months. Most of the scholars hold the opinion that this night is amongst the unique blessings that Allah ﷻ has granted only to the *Umma* of the Prophet Muhammad ﷺ. No other community before us was granted anything like this. A hadith narrated by Anas ؓ also supports this opinion. It reads:

إِنَّ اللهَ وَهَبَ لِأُمَّتِي لَيْلَةَ الْقَدْرِ، وَلَمْ يُعْطِهَا مَنْ كَانَ قَبْلَكُمْ.

'Allah has undoubtedly granted the Night of Destiny to my *Umma* and has never given it to those before you.'[166]

Since it has been established through many hadiths, that it falls within the odd nights during the last ten days of Ramaḍān, we should search it amongst those nights.

Q.117. What superiority does the Night of Destiny possess over other nights?

A: Allah ﷻ has revealed one complete chapter in the Qur'ān to express the high merits attached to this night. The chapter states:

﴿إِنَّآ أَنزَلْنَٰهُ فِى لَيْلَةِ ٱلْقَدْرِ. وَمَآ أَدْرَىٰكَ مَا لَيْلَةُ ٱلْقَدْرِ. لَيْلَةُ ٱلْقَدْرِ خَيْرٌ مِّنْ أَلْفِ شَهْرٍ. تَنَزَّلُ ٱلْمَلَٰٓئِكَةُ وَٱلرُّوحُ فِيهَا بِإِذْنِ رَبِّهِم مِّن كُلِّ أَمْرٍ. سَلَٰمٌ هِىَ حَتَّىٰ مَطْلَعِ ٱلْفَجْرِ﴾

Surely We sent down this (Holy Qur'ān) during the Night of Destiny. And what have you made out what the Night of Destiny is? The Night of Destiny is better than a thousand months (in merit of excellence, blessings, reward and recompense). The angels and the Spirit of Peace

---

[166] Narrated by al-Daylamī in *al-Firdaws bi Ma'thūr al-Khiṭāb*, 1:173 §647.

(Gabriel) descend by their Lord's Command during this (night) with decrees concerning all matters (of blessings and bounties). This (night) is (absolute) peace and security till daybreak.[167]

There is a great number of hadiths on this matter. Below, we mention some of them.

1. Abū Hurayra ﷺ reported that the Prophet ﷺ said:

مَنْ قَامَ لَيْلَةَ الْقَدْرِ إِيْمَانًا وَاحْتِسَابًا غُفِرَ لَهُ مَا تَقَدَّمَ مِنْ ذَنْبِهِ.

> 'Whoever stands (in worship) during the Night of Destiny in the state of *īmān* and with the intention of reward, will have all his previous sins forgiven.'[168]

This hadith not only places emphasis upon remembrance, contemplation, obedience and worship in order to take full advantage of the blessings concealed within the moments of this night, it also draws our attention to the importance of purity and the sincerity of intention behind our worship. Our actions should not be done for show, but for the good pleasure of Allah ﷻ. Action should also accompany the resolve not to commit an evil deed again. The worshippers with this quality receive the glad tidings of forgiveness, by means of this night. Unfortunate are those who find this night and fail to decorate it with worship.

2. Anas b. Mālik ﷺ reported that the Prophet ﷺ once said as Ramaḍān approached,

> 'This month that has just come to you contains a night superior to one thousand months. Whoever fails to find it is bereft of all good. Only the real

---

[167] Qur'ān, *al-Qadr*, 97:1–5.

[168] Narrated by al-Bukhārī in *al-Ṣaḥīḥ*, 2:709 §1910.

> loser can remain deprived of the good of this night.'[169]

Who can doubt the loss of the person who loses a blessing of such magnitude, for no other reason than heedlessness? Keeping awake for one night whose worship is superior to the worship of one thousand months could not be deemed hard, for those who can stay up for night upon night just for some trivial worldly benefit.

3. Anas ﷺ reported that the Prophet ﷺ expressed the significance of the Night of Destiny in the following words:

> 'On this night, Jibrīl descends upon the earth in the midst of a multitude of angels and seeks forgiveness for each person remembering Allah, ﷻ sitting or standing (in any condition).'[170]

Q.118. What are the odd nights of the ten last days of Ramaḍān?

A: They are the 21st, 23rd, 25th, 27th and 29th nights of Ramaḍān. ʿUbāda b. al-Ṣāmit ﷺ reports that he asked the Prophet ﷺ about the Night of Destiny. The Prophet ﷺ replied:

فِي رَمَضَانَ، فَالْتَمِسُوْهَا فِي الْعَشْرِ الْأَوَاخِرِ فَإِنَّهَا وِتْرٌ، فِي إِحْدَى وَعِشْرِيْنَ أَوْ ثَلَاثٍ وَعِشْرِيْنَ أَوْ خَمْسٍ وَعِشْرِيْنَ أَوْ سَبْعٍ وَعِشْرِيْنَ أَوْ تِسْعٍ وَعِشْرِيْنَ أَوْ فِي آخِرِ لَيْلَةٍ، فَمَنْ قَامَهَا ابْتِغَاءَهَا إِيْمَانًا وَاحْتِسَابًا ثُمَّ وُفِّقَتْ لَهُ، غُفِرَ لَهُ مَا تَقَدَّمَ مِنْ ذَنْبِهِ.

> 'In Ramaḍān, search it in the last ten days. It is the 21st or 23rd or 25th or 27th or 29th or the last

---

[169] Narrated by Ibn Mājah in *al-Sunan*, 2:309 §1644.

[170] Narrated by al-Bayhaqī in *Shuʿab al-Īmān*, 3:343 §3717.

night (of Ramaḍān). Whoever stands in (prayer for) them searching for it in the state of *īmān* and with the intention of its reward, then he is enabled with the grace of capturing it (particular moments of acceptance and) his previous and forthcoming sins are forgiven.'[171]

Q.119. What is the wisdom behind keeping the Night of Destiny hidden?

A: Like other significant hidden matters such as the Exalted Name of the Almighty (ineffable word—*al-ism al-aʿẓam*) and the moment of acceptance on Fridays, there are a number of reasons that the Night of Destiny has been concealed. We mention some of them here:

- Disclosing it would close the door of works. People would be content with only one, that particular one night's worship. So, it has not been disclosed in order to grant the fervour of worship permanence.
- To bear the trauma of having lost it would be impossible, for those who might lose it under some obligation (for they are now sure they have lost it).
- Allah ﷻ loves for His worshipful servants to stay awake at night and busy themselves with acts of worship. One of the reasons it has not been specified is to motivate them to worship for at least five nights and please their Lord.
- Another reason is mercy for the sinners. If somebody knew it and still committed some sin in it, it would be a deliberate disrespect to this night. Offending the honour of such a night is definitely a serious sin.

---

[171] Narrated by Aḥmad b. Ḥanbal in *al-Musnad*, 5:319 §22713.

Q.120. Which supplication has been prescribed by the Prophet ﷺ for this night?

A: Mother of the Believers ʿĀʾisha ﵂ reports that she once asked the Prophet ﷺ what supplication she should make if she found the Night of Destiny. The Prophet ﷺ told her to say:

اَللَّهُمَّ إِنَّكَ عَفُوٌّ، تُحِبُّ الْعَفْوَ، فَاعْفُ عَنِّي.

> 'O Allah! You are Oft-Forgiving; love to forgive; so please, forgive me.'[172]

---

[172] Narrated by al-Tirmidhī in *al-Sunan*, 5:490 §3513.

6. Rulings regarding Spiritual Retreat

Q.121. Is it a requisite of spiritual retreat founded on the Prophetic practice to include fasting?

A: Yes, it is conditional on fasting. Spiritual retreat founded on the Prophetic practice is not valid without fasting. This is the reason a woman is not supposed to perform either a fast or spiritual retreat during her monthly periods.

Q.122. Is *al-qaḍā*ʾ necessary for somebody who leaves spiritual retreat in the middle?

A:

- In case of optional spiritual retreat, no *al-qaḍā*ʾ is necessary.
- In case of spiritual retreat founded on the Prophetic practice, which is done during last ten days of Ramaḍān, one does not have to make *al-qaḍā*ʾ (recompense) for all ten days or for the days he has completed, but for the days he has left out and those he left incomplete.
- In case of imperative spiritual retreat, one would have to recompense for the day he has left out completely or partly if he has taken a vow for a certain number of days, or for a month or week, etc.

- He would recompense for all the days for which he had taken vow, if the vow was that of spiritual retreat for consecutive days.

Q.123. What is the way to make *al-qaḍāʾ* for one day spiritual retreat?

A:

- One must enter the mosque for spiritual retreat before the break of dawn and leave it after sunset if he has broken the spiritual retreat during the day.
- In the case of breaking spiritual retreat at night, one must start before sunset and end after the sunset of the following day, a little over 24 hours.

He must keep fast during the day in both cases.

Q.124. After having broken the spiritual retreat founded on the Prophetic practice, can a person continue with his spiritual retreat with the intention of optional spiritual retreat?

A: If spiritual retreat founded on the Prophetic practice has been broken, he does not have to leave the mosque, although his spiritual retreat has been broken and cannot be completed by staying. On the other hand, he can continue to stay there with the intention of optional seclusion, which can remain valid. He also has the option to leave the mosque, if he cannot continue there. Or he can leave the mosque that day and return for optional spiritual retreat the following day.

Q.125. Under what circumstances can a man break his spiritual retreat?

A: There are four situations where *al-muʿtakif* can break his spiritual retreat:

Illness

If a person gets ill during spiritual retreat and the illness requires urgent attention or treatment, which is impossible without going out of the place of spiritual retreat, he is allowed to break spiritual retreat.

Illness of parents, children or wife

If the father, mother, wife or children of *al-muʿtakif* is taken by some severe illness or injured by a serious accident and there is nobody to look after them, one is allowed to break his spiritual retreat and attend the patient.

Funeral

If any close relations such as parents, or a brother or sister dies suddenly and there is no one else to perform the funeral rites and ceremonies, one can break his spiritual retreat to pay proper respect to the deceased.

Driven out forcefully

If *al-muʿtakif* is forced out of the mosque or is arrested by the authorities, it will break his spiritual retreat but he will not incur any sin for breaking it.

Q.126. What are spiritual retreat-nullifiers?

A: The following things break spiritual retreat:

- Exiting the mosque without a valid excuse
- Coition during spiritual retreat
- Commencement of menstruation or post-natal bleeding

- Remaining outside the mosque longer than necessary, in case one has to go out for valid reason.

All these things break spiritual retreat.

Q.127. WHAT ARE THE DISLIKES IN SPIRITUAL RETREAT?

A: The dislikes (al-makrūhāt) in spiritual retreat include the following things:

To adopt a complete silence. If one believes that keeping silent is an act of worship, in contrast with speaking in the course of al-da'wa, al-dhikr and al-nashīd, it would amount to al-makrūh al-taḥrīmī (i.e., nearly unlawful). If one keeps quiet to avoid any useless worldly talk, it is an act of righteousness.

To involve oneself with trade, by bringing merchandise inside the mosque and selling and buying there.

Quarrelling, arguing or bad-mouthing.

Q.128. CAN AL-MU'TAKIF MOVE TO ANOTHER MOSQUE FOR COMPLETING HIS SPIRITUAL RETREAT IN A DESPERATE SITUATION?

A: Yes, he can. For example if his life is in danger in the mosque where he started spiritual retreat, or the mosque is in the process of destruction. In such a case, one must leave for another mosque with the quickest speed possible.

Q.129. CAN AL-MU'TAKIF GO OUT TO INQUIRE AFTER A SICK PERSON'S HEALTH OR TO ATTEND A FUNERAL PRAYER?

A: No, he cannot. 'Ā'isha 🙏 says:

> 'It is Sunna for al-mu'takif not to go out to inquire after an ill person; to attend a funeral

> prayer; to touch his wife (with sexual desire) or to have coition; to attend a need unnecessarily (not accepted as valid excuse).'[173]

Only when a person is out for a valid reason, he can inquire after somebody's health if he happens to pass by him and without having stopped walking. ʿĀʾisha ﵂ herself narrates:

كَانَ النَّبِيُّ ﷺ بِالْمَرِيْضِ وَهُوَ مُعْتَكِفٌ ، فَيَمُرُّ كَمَا هُوَ وَلَا يُعَرِّجُ يَسْأَلُ عَنْهُ.

وَقَالَ التِّرْمِذِيُّ: قَالَتْ: إِنْ كَانَ النَّبِيُّ ﷺ يَعُودُ الْـمَرِيْضَ وَهُوَ مُعتَكِفٌ.

> 'The holy Prophet ﷺ would inquire after a sick person while passing by (and without having stopped), if he was *al-muʿtakif* (and happened to go out of the mosque for his need).'
>
> Al-Tirmidhī says that ʿĀʾisha ﵂ said that the Prophet ﷺ would inquire after the sick person's health during spiritual retreat.[174]

This shows that a person is not allowed to leave the mosque with the intention of attending a funeral prayer or inquiring after a sick person's health, because it will break his spiritual retreat.

If however, he has included these visits while making intention for spiritual retreat, going out when extreme circumstances demand it, will not break his spiritual retreat.

---

[173] Narrated by Abū Dawūd in *al-Sunan*, 2:333 §2473.
[174] Narrated by Abū Dawūd in *al-Sunan*, 2:333 §2472.

Q.130. What can legitimise *al-muʿtakif* going out of the mosque?

A: *Al-Muʿtakif* can go outside the mosque building to attend the call of nature and to take an imperative major ritual bath, if the facility is not available in the premises. Likewise, one can also attend Friday prayer if the facility is not available in the mosque where he performs spiritual retreat. The same is true if he needs to attend a funeral prayer, if he made the intention of doing so as he started his spiritual retreat. But it is most important for him to return to the mosque of his spiritual retreat, as soon as the need is done. If the need for which he is out takes longer than half a day, it will break his spiritual retreat (so, it is also important to leave aside the need if it takes longer than that).

Q.131. Are we allowed to have a shower during spiritual retreat?

A: Yes, if the facility is available on the premises, be it imperative or not.

Q.132. If a person starts Ramaḍān in Saudi Arabia which happens to be two days prior to the start in Pakistan. He reaches Pakistan on the 8th of Ramaḍān and has fasted ten days. Now he wants to perform spiritual retreat. On what day should he start (18th or 22nd according to his counting of fasts in another country)?

A: If a person starts his Ramaḍān while in Saudi Arabia because he was there when it started, it means he has found Ramaḍān two days earlier than in Pakistan for example, where he arrived later in Ramaḍān. Allah ﷻ says:

(فَمَن شَهِدَ مِنكُمُ ٱلشَّهْرَ فَلْيَصُمْهُ)

Therefore, he who witnesses this month must fast it.[175]

It is definite that spiritual retreat founded on the Prophetic practice cannot be more than ten days and the days of Ramaḍān cannot exceed 30. So, he must start his spiritual retreat on the 18th of Ramaḍān in Pakistan, which would be his 20th day of fasting, based on the date he started it. He will complete his spiritual retreat on the 28th of Ramaḍān, for Ramaḍān cannot have more than 30 days. He will not fast the next day, the 29th in Pakistan but can observe optional spiritual retreat if he wants to.

ʿAbd Allāh b. ʿUmar ؓ says that the Prophet ﷺ said as he mentioned Ramaḍān.

لَا تَصُوْمُوا حَتَّى تَرَوُا الْهِلَالَ ، وَلَا تُفْطِرُوا حَتَّى تَرَوْهُ، فَإِنْ أُغْمِيَ عَلَيْكُمْ فَاقْدِرُوْا لَهُ.

'Do not fast until you sight the crescent and do not break fast until you sight it. If it is cloudy for you then count it fully (make it the month of 30 days).'[176]

So, it is important to start the month where you have sighted the moon and complete 30 days when you are in a different country, where the moon is not visible, when you complete your 29th fast, for no lunar month can have more than 30 days.

---

[175] Qurʾān, *al-Baqara*, 2:185.

[176] Narrated by Muslim in *al-Ṣaḥīḥ*, 4:759 §1080.

Q.133. In the case of collective spiritual retreat, is the spiritual retreat of those accommodated in the rooms next to the mosque and in the tents set on the piece of land adjacent to it, valid?

A: Basically, spiritual retreat is performed inside a mosque. If the number of secluded persons exceeds the space available within the mosque, buildings and classrooms adjacent to the mosque are also declared to be part of the mosque. It is just like using the buildings and classrooms as a mosque in many religious educational institutes, if the number of performers of congregational prayers cannot be contained within the mosque itself. This is also true in the case of ordinary mosques when the number of those performing their prayers overflows, the main building on particular occasions such as *ʿīd* or Friday, etc. In such situations, even the surrounding roads are also covered with the congregation.

Abū Hurayra ﵁ reported that the Prophet ﷺ said,

> 'I have been granted privilege above all other Prophets by six; I have been granted comprehensive words; I have been assisted with awe; spoils of war have been made permissible for me; the whole Earth has been purified and made a lawful place of worship; I have been sent to the whole creation as Messenger; and the Prophethood has been finalised with me (i.e., I am the last Prophet).'[177]

So, the entire place adjacent to the mosque takes the character of the mosque itself, for those performing their prayers with the congregation and this earns everyone

---

[177] Narrated by Ibn Ḥibbān in *al-Ṣaḥīḥ*, 14:311 §6451.

who joins the congregation while still outside the mosque, the same reward as those inside the mosque.

By the grace of Allah ﷻ, the partakers of spiritual retreat in Minhaj-ul-Quran are in the five figures. All those sons of Islam and self-immolating lovers of the holy Prophet ﷺ can no longer fit within the hall of the mosque. Based on the rule of necessity, the entire place adjacent to the mosque, rooms as well as a vast yard, take the character of the vicinity of the mosque. So, the spiritual retreat (*al-iʿtikāf*) of all those people is valid.

Q.134. Are women allowed to perform spiritual retreat?

A: Yes, they can. The wives of the Prophet ﷺ used to do so. Mother of the Believers ʿĀʾishah ﵂ said,

> 'The Holy Prophet ﷺ would perform spiritual retreat during the last ten days of Ramaḍān until his communion with His Lord. His wives continued to do so after his demise.'[178]

Q.135. Can a woman perform spiritual retreat without her husband's permission?

A: No, she is not allowed to do so.

Q.136. Where could a woman sit for spiritual retreat?

A: The best option for a woman is confined to the place specified for prayer at home, which is known as 'the mosque of the house'.

[178] Narrated by al-Bukhārī in *al-Ṣaḥīḥ*, 2:713 §1922.

Q.137. Are women allowed to sit for spiritual retreat at a place distant from home?

A: Yes, they can do so provided that regular arrangements to insure their veil, privacy, security, moral well-being, education, self-purification and spiritual cleansing are made. Thousands of men and women in many big mosques and Islamic education centres, do sit for *al-iʿtikāf*-retreat with well-assured segregation, privacy and security. They are given a well-managed timetable for their daily course of deeds. Although we do not argue that fulfilling all the requisites is possible in every mosque.

About the issue of a woman sitting for *al-iʿtikāf*-retreat in a mosque, Ibn Nujaym al-Ḥanafī writes:

إِنَّ اعْتِكَافَهَا فِي مَسْجِدِ الْجَمَاعَةِ جَائِزٌ.

> The spiritual retreat of a woman in a mosque of congregation (where the five daily prayers are regularly held) is allowed beyond doubt.

He further writes with quoting al-Kāsānī from *Badāʾiʿ al-Ṣānāʾiʿ*:

إِنَّ اعْتِكَافَهَا فِي مَسْجِدِ الْجَمَاعَةِ صَحِيْحٌ بِلَا خِلَافٍ بَيْنَ أَصْحَابِنَا.

> Her *iʿtikāf* in the mosque of congregation is undoubtedly valid, without a single opinion amongst our scholars to differ.[179]

Ibn ʿĀbidīn al-Shāmī, in his book *Rad al-Muḥtār* (2:441) declares her sitting for spiritual retreat in a mosque *al-makrūh al-tanzīhī*.[180] He also quotes *Badāʾiʿ al-Ṣānāʾiʿ*:

---

[179] Ibn Nujaym al-Ḥanafī, *al-Baḥr al-Rāʾiq*, 2:324.
[180] That which approaches the lawful.

صُرِّحَ فِي الْبَدَائِعِ أَنَّهُ خِلَافُ الْأَفْضَلِ.

> It is clearly stated in *al-Badāʾiʿ* that it is against the preferable.

It means that her spiritual retreat at home is preferable to the mosque.Here it is important to mention that not every mosque can make proper arrangements for women's spiritual retreat and this is the basis of the prohibition against it. A mosque, if spacious enough to accommodate both men and women with all the requisites of segregation, and capable enough to enforce a routine of educational and spiritual purification through a timetable of optional prayers along with the obligations, sending of greetings and salutation to the Prophet ﷺ, *al-dhikr*, admonition, advice and regular invocations, can enhance the prospect of benefit and reward to a far higher degree, as compared to the individual/private activity of spiritual retreat.

The collective spiritual retreat held at the centre of Minhaj-ul-Quran is an example of this, where both male and female attendants from far and near, prosper with spiritual training. Women travel all the way to the place of spiritual retreat with their husbands or some other member of their family such as brothers or fathers or grandfathers etc., where a spacious area adjacent to the mosque is made available for their accommodation and meals in complete segregation from men. In order to serve them there and make their stay as comfortable and easy as possible, hundreds of young female students from Minhaj Girls' College and senior members of the Minhaj Women's League, take charge inside the building. Armed guards are also appointed at the doors. All the attendants are registered. A 24/7 presence of lady doctors, paramedics and teams of first aid helpers is charged to deal with illness and accidents. The volunteers also include those responsible for cleanliness in the premises. Regular educational circles for learning the Qur'ān, hadith, fiqh and tasawwuf are in place. All this is neither possible nor available at every place. Their importance does not need stressing. We can also refer back to question number 114.

Q.138. Can a woman sit for spiritual retreat and use tablets or injection to stop the valid excuse (her monthly cycle, for example) for the purpose?

A: Yes, provided that it does not harm her health (i.e. it does not have any side-effects). She can only use them from dusk to dawn (only at night). But her spiritual retreat will still be broken if she happens to have it, even for a few seconds.

Q.139. If a woman's spiritual retreat breaks for valid excuse (her monthly cycle, for example), how many days shall she make *al-qaḍā'*?

A: If a woman happens to break her spiritual retreat for some valid excuse such as becoming ill, starting menstruation, giving birth or remaining outside the place of spiritual retreat for longer than permitted, she will make the *qaḍā'* for all the days left including the day she broke it (if it happened during the day). If she has missed the (same number of) fasts too, it is more appropriate to do them both together. Or else, she will add optional fasts to *al-qaḍā'* of spiritual retreat.

7. *ĪD AL-FIṬR* AND *ṢADAQA AL-FIṬR*

Q.140. WHEN WAS THE PRAYER OF TWO *ʿĪDS* OBLIGATED?

A: It was obligated during the first year of hegira. Allah ﷻ granted Muslims two days to celebrate; namely *ʿĪd al-Fiṭr* and *ʿĪd al-Aḍḥā*. Anas ﷺ reports when the Prophet ﷺ arrived at Medina, the people there used to spend two days playing around. When asked they said they were the days of playing around in the days of ignorance. The Prophet ﷺ said:

إِنَّ اللهَ قَدْ أَبْدَلَكُمْ بِهِمَا خَيْرًا مِنْهُمَا؛ يَوْمُ الْأَضْحَى وَيَوْمُ الْفِطْرِ.

> 'Allah ﷻ has exchanged these two days with two days better than these; the day of *al-Aḍḥā* and the day of *al-Fiṭr*.'[181]

Q.141. WHY HAS *ĪD AL-FIṬR* BEEN REGARDED AS THE DAY OF HAPPINESS?

A: This day combines a number of matters that bring joy and happiness. They include the happiness of fasting in Ramaḍān, the night vigil, the descent of the Qurʾān, Night of Destiny and deliverance from perdition. It is further required to express rejoicing by the charitable act of imperative offering of *ṣadaqa al-Fiṭr*[182], which includes

[181] Narrated by Abū Dawūd in *al-Sunan*, 1:295 §1134.
[182] Obligatory alms given at the end of the month of Ramaḍān and before the prayer of *ʿīd al-Fiṭr*.

the act of charity as an essential part of worship. These are a few reasons to make it a day of rejoicing.

Q.142. ARE WE ALLOWED TO FAST ON ʿĪD DAY?

A: No, we are not. Our Prophet ﷺ has forbidden us to do so. Abū Saʿīd al-Khudrī ؓ said:

نَهَى رَسُوْلُ اللهِ ﷺ عَنْ صِيَامِ يَوْمَيْنِ: يَوْمِ الْفِطْرِ وَيَوْمِ الْأَضْحَى.

'Allah's Messenger ﷺ has forbidden fasting on two days; the day of al-Fiṭr and the day of al-Aḍḥā.'[183]

Q.143. WHAT IS THE TIME OF PRAYER OF ʿĪD AL-FIṬR? CAN IT BE DELAYED?

A: The time of the prayer of ʿīd starts after the sun rises and ends before midday, the exact point between the break of dawn and sunset. We are allowed to delay it from its start time in case of ʿĪd al-Fiṭr. Our beloved Prophet ﷺ directed ʿAmr b. Ḥazm ؓ in Najrān as follows:

عَجِّلِ الْأَضْحَى وَأَخِّرِ الْفِطْرَ وَذَكِّرِ النَّاسَ.

'Hasten the prayer of al-Aḍḥa; delay the prayer of al-Fiṭr; and deliver a reminder (sermon).'[184]

Q.144. WHAT IS THE RULING ABOUT THE ADHĀN AND IQĀMA FOR THE PRAYER OF ʿĪD?

A. There is no al-adhān or al-iqāma for the prayer of ʿīd. Jabir b. ʿAbd Allāh ؓ said:

---

[183] Narrated by Abū Dawūd in al-Sunan, 2:314 §2417.
[184] Narrated by al-Bayhaqī in al-Sunan al-Kubrā, 3:282 §5944.

شَهِدْتُ مَعَ رَسُوْلِ اللهِ ﷺ الصَّلَاةَ يَوْمَ الْعِيْدِ، فَبَدَأَ بِالصَّلَاةِ قَبْلَ الْخُطْبَةِ بِغَيْرِ أَذَانٍ وَلَا إِقَامَةٍ.

'I attended the prayer of *ʿīd* with Allah's Messenger ﷺ. He started the prayer prior to sermon without *al-adhān* and *al-iqāma*.'[185]

Q.145. How do we perform the prayer of *ʿĪd*?

A: *ʿĪd* prayer is obligated upon everyone who is subject to the obligation of Friday prayer. It consist of two cycles and is offered the way any other two-cycles-prayer would be offered, with the difference of six additional *takbīrāt*.[186] The Imam recites *al-thanāʾ* after the first *al-takbīr* (*takbīr taḥrīma*), and then says three additional *al-takbīrāt* raising his hands each time. After the third *takbīr*, he places his hands under his navel. The Imam recites the chapter *al-Fātiḥa* and another chapter loudly, after reading *al-taʿawwudh* and *al-tasmiya* and then performs bowing (*al-rukūʿ*) and prostrations (*al-sujūd*) as usual. In the second cycle, the Imam recites the chapter *al-Fātiḥa* and another chapter and then says three additional *al-takbīrāt,* raising his hands each time. Then he says the fourth *al-takbīr* without raising his hands and goes to *al-rukuʿ*. Then he completes the rest of the second cycle as usual. The followers follow him from start to finish.

Q.146. What things are established by the Prophetic practice and what are commendable on the day of *ʿĪd*?

A: Following things are commendable on *ʿīd* days.

- Cleanliness of teeth (use of twig is Sunna)

[185] Narrated by Muslim in *al-Ṣaḥīḥ*, 2:603 §885.

[186] Utterance of the phrase *Allāhu Akbar*.

- To have bath
- To wear clean and washed clothes, if new ones cannot be afforded
- Wearing perfume
- Preparing to go to the place of *ʿīd* prayer.
- Paying *ṣadaqa al-Fiṭr* before offering the prayer of *al-Fiṭr*
- Going to the place of *ʿīd* prayer on foot
- Choosing a different way back to the one taken there
- Eating dates, fresh or dry, or something sweet before leaving for the prayer of *ʿīd*
- Not to eat anything before the prayer of *ʿīd* on the day of *al-Aḍḥā*. After the prayer, it is commendable to eat from the meat of sacrifice as the first thing of the day, if available. Eating something else would not be a sin though.
- It is Sunna to perform the prayer of *ʿīd* in a vast field. In big cities and towns with extensive populations, though, *ʿīd* congregations without the condition of a vast field are also allowed. Congregations in huge mosques as we have them today are also allowed. The reason for this permission is that if the condition of one vast field were applied today, a great number of prayer-offerers would be unable to perform it, for reasons either of practical difficulty or personal laziness.
- Reciting *al-takbīr* of *tashrīq Allāhu akbaru-llāhu Akbar, lā ilāha illa-llāhu wa-llāhu akbar, Allāhu akbar, wa li-llāh-il-ḥamd* while heading towards the place of prayer; loudly on the day of *al-Aḍḥā* and secretly on the day of *al-Fiṭr*.
- The sermons for both the *ʿīds* is Sunna. It is supposed to occur after the prayer.

• It is reprehensible (al-makrūh) to deliver the sermon before ʿīd prayer. If somebody has done so, revising it is not required.

Q.147. WHAT ARE THE MERITS OF WORSHIP DURING ʿĪD NIGHT?

A: The reward of the worship performed during the night of ʿīd and its merits are many times greater than that of any other day. Abū Umāma ☙ reported the Prophet ﷺ to have said:

$$مَنْ قَامَ لَيْلَتَي الْعِيْدَيْنِ مُـ ـحْتَسِبًا للهِ، لَمْ يَمُتْ قَلْبُهُ يَوْمَ تَـمُوْتُ الْقُلُوْبُ.$$

‘Whoever stands at the nights of the two ʿīds with the intention of reward, will not have his heart dead the day hearts die.’[187]

Muʿādh b. Jabal ☙ reported the Prophet ﷺ to have said:

$$مَنْ أَحْيَا اللَّيَالِي الْخَمْسَ، وَجَبَتْ لَهُ الْـجَنَّةُ: لَيْلَةُ التَّرْوِيَةِ وَلَيْلَةُ عَرَفَةَ وَلَيْلَةُ النَّحْرِ وَلَيْلَةُ الْفِطْرِ وَلَيْلَةُ النِّصْفِ مِنْ شَعْبَانَ.$$

‘Paradise is confirmed for whoever livens (with worship) five nights (with worship); the night of the eighth, ninth and tenth of Dhū al-Ḥijja, the night of ʿĪd al-Fiṭr and the fifteenth night of Shaʿbān.’[188]

---

[187] Narrated by Ibn Mājah in al-Sunan, 2:377 §1782.
[188] Narrated by al-Mundhirī in al-Targhīb wa al-Tarhīb, 1:182.

Q.148. What is *Ṣadaqa al-Fiṭr*?

A: It is the disbursement our beloved Prophet ﷺ commanded when the fast of Ramaḍān was obligated, one year prior to the obligation of Zakat. It is given to the poor and needy. It behoves every wealthy person to practise it, so that the needy may also join in the ʿ*Īd* rejoicings. *Ṣadaqa al-Fiṭr* is also an important means of purifying the one who has fasted, from useless and indecent deeds.

Ibn ʿAbbās رضي الله عنه says that our beloved Prophet ﷺ has obligated *ṣadaqa al-Fiṭr* because it safeguards the one who fasts from useless and indecent deeds, as well as being a source of food for the needy.[189]

Q.149. Who is *Ṣadaqa al-Fiṭr* obligated upon?

A: It is obligated upon all Muslims who can afford it. Ibn ʿUmar رضي الله عنه says:

فَرَضَ رَسُوْلُ اللهِ ﷺ زَكَاةَ الْفِطْرِ مِنْ رَمَضَانَ، صَاعًا مِنْ تَمْرٍ أَوْ صَاعًا مِنْ شَعِيْرٍ، عَلَى الْعَبْدِ وَالْحُرِّ، وَالذَّكَرِ وَالْأُنْثَى، وَالصَّغِيْرِ وَالْكَبِيْرِ مِنَ الْمُسْلِمِيْنَ.

> 'Allah's Messenger ﷺ obligated the Zakat of *al-Fiṭr* (from Ramaḍān) upon every slave and free male and female and minor and major amongst Muslims. It is 3261.5 grams of dates or barley.'[190]

Abū Hurayra رضي الله عنه also reports the Prophet ﷺ to have said,

---

[189] Narrated by Abū Dawūd in *al-Sunan*, 2:28 §1609.
[190] Narrated by al-Bukhārī in *al-Ṣaḥīḥ*, 2:547 §1432.

> '*Ṣadaqa al-Fiṭr* behoves every person wealthy-in-Shariah.'[191]

A wealthy-in-Shariah person is a person upon whom Zakat has been obligated. Or at least one with enough in cash or kind or both including his house and household, to obligate Zakat if it was in surplus of basic needs. *Ṣadaqa al-Fiṭr* is an obligation, whether a whole year has passed or not, or if it is merchandise or not.

Q.150. What is the most suitable time for paying *Ṣadaqa al-Fiṭr*?

A: The best time to pay *ṣadaqa al-Fiṭr* is between the break of dawn and offering *ʿīd* prayer. Our beloved Prophet ﷺ has recommended paying it prior to leaving for *ʿīd* prayer.[192]

If somebody could not pay it on the day of *ʿīd*, he must pay it as soon as it becomes possible for him. It will not become *al-qaḍāʾ*. It will still be *al-adāʾ*.

Q.151. What are the benefits of *Ṣadaqa al-Fiṭr*?

A: The following are the main benefits of *ṣadaqa al-Fiṭr*.

- It earns us the reward of acting upon a command of the Shariah.
- It is a means to purify the fast from any shortcomings.
- It ensures support for the needy on the day of *ʿīd*. This is why it should be made prior to *ʿīd* prayer.

---

[191] Narrated by al-Kinānī in *Zujāja al-Maṣābīḥ*, 1:115.

[192] Narrated by al-Bukhārī in *al-Ṣaḥīḥ*, 2:548 §1438.

Q.152. What are the merits of charitable deeds (*al-ṣadaqāt*) during Ramaḍān?

A: *Al-Ṣadaqa* is the wealth spent upon the poor and the needy for the sake of Allah's good pleasure. Its three forms, namely Zakat, *al-ᶜushr* and *ṣadaqa al-Fiṭr*, fall under the category of the imperative. Whoever does not pay any of them is seriously rendered sinful. Other forms of *al-ṣadaqa* also earn us a great deal of blessing and reward. It carries limitless benefits in this world and in the hereafter. In Ramaḍān, nevertheless, it increases to the highest of levels. Below, we mention a couple of the hadiths to express its merits during Ramaḍān.

Anas b. Mālik ﵁ reports that the Prophet ﷺ said when he was asked about the best of *al-ṣadaqa*,

> '*Al-Ṣadaqa* in Ramaḍān is the best rewardable *al-ṣadaqa*.'[193]

ᶜAbd Allāh b. ᶜAbbās ﵄ reports that the Prophet ﷺ was the most generous person. His generosity would increase in Ramaḍān, as he would meet Jibrīl. At that point, his generosity would increase more than that of unrestricted wind (which reaches everybody).'[194]

8. Rulings of Shariah regarding *ᶜĪd al-Fiṭr* and *Ṣadaqa al-Fiṭr*

Q.153. Is congregation a prerequisite for *ᶜĪd* prayer?

A: Yes, it is a precondition for *ᶜīd* prayer. Even one person behind the imām validates the prayer.

---

[193] Narrated by al-Tirmidhī in *al-Sunan*, 2:43 §663.

[194] Narrated by al-Bukhārī in *al-Ṣaḥīḥ*, 2:672 §1803.

Q.154. What is the procedure of delivering the *ʿĪd* sermon?

A: After completing the prayer of *ʿīd* with greetings, the Imam stands up on the lowest step of the pulpit facing the audience, without having supplicated. Now he recites a *al-taʿawwudh* and then *al-tasmiya* secretly. Then he says *al-takbīr* nine times or says the *al-takbīr* of *al-tashrīq Allāhu akbaru-llāhu Akbar, lā ilāha illa-llāhu wa-llāhu akbar, Allāhu akbar, wa li-llāh-il-ḥamd* three times. Then he starts delivering the sermon.

At the end of the first sermon, he sits down for as long as he can say *subhān Allāh* three times or recite three small verses from the Qurʾān. Then he stands up again and says *al-takbīr* seven times or *al-takbīr* of *al-tashrīq* twice. Now he starts the second sermon.

Q.155. If somebody misses the *ʿĪd* prayer or it is broken or nullified for some reason, does he have to make *al-qaḍāʾ* for that?

A: No, he does not have to make *al-qaḍāʾ* for it if he missed the Imam or happened to nullify it for some reason. However, if he wants to offer the prayer of *al-ḍuḥā*, without additional *al-takbīrāt*, he can do that. He will recite the chapter *al-Aʿlā* in the first cycle, chapter *al-Ḍuḥā* in the second cycle, chapter *al-Inshirāḥ* in the third cycle and chapter *al-Tīn* in the last cycle.

Q.156. What is the ruling of offering Friday prayer if *¢¬d* happens to be on that day?

A: In this case, both the prayers will be offered at their regular time as usual. The blessings and benevolence of Allah will be doubled.

Abū Ṣāliḥ al-Zayyāt narrates:

إِنَّ النَّبِيَّ ﷺ اجْتَمَعَ فِي زَمَانِهِ يَوْمَ جُمُعَةٍ وَيَوْمَ فِطْرٍ، فَقَالَ: إِنَّ هَذَا الْيَوْمَ يَوْمٌ قَدِ اجْتَمَعَ فِيهِ عِيدَانِ، فَمَنْ أَحَبَّ فَلْيَنْقَلِبْ وَمَنْ أَحَبَّ أَنْ يَنْتَظِرَ فَلْيَنْتَظِرْ.

'Once, when the *ʿīd* day fell on Friday, the Prophet ﷺ said, 'Today is a day when two *ʿīds* have arrived together. So, whoso wants to return (home after *ʿīd* prayer to come back later for Friday prayer) can return; and whoso wants to remain here waiting (for the Friday prayer) is allowed to wait here.''[195]

The freed-slave of ʿAbd al-Raḥmān b. ʿAwf ؓ, Abū ʿUbayd ؓ reports that he was with ʿUthmān ؓ when *ʿĪd al-Fiṭr* fell on a Friday. ʿUthmān ؓ delivered the *ʿīd* sermon and then said:

فَمَنْ كَانَ مِنْ أَهْلِ الْعَوَالِي فَأَحَبَّ أَنْ يَمْكُثَ حَتَّى يَشْهَدَ الْجُمُعَةَ فَلْيَفْعَلْ، وَمَنْ أَحَبَّ أَنْ يَنْصَرِفَ فَقَدْ أَذِنَّا لَهُ.

'Whoso belongs to the highlands (of Medina, here meaning the outskirts of the city therefore too distant from the city to obligate Friday prayer) and wants to stay behind to attend Friday prayer can do so; and whoso wants to return (home) we permit him to do so.'[196]

Nuʿmān b. Bashīr ؓ narrates:

---

[195] Narrated by ʿAbd al-Razzāq in *al-Muṣannaf*, 3:304 §5729.
[196] Narrated by ʿAbd al-Razzāq in *al-Muṣannaf*, 3:305 §5732.

كَانَ رَسُوْلُ اللهِ ﷺ يَقْرَأُ فِي الْجُمُعَةِ وَالْعِيْدِ بِـ ﴿سَبِّحِ اسْمَ رَبِّكَ الْأَعْلَى﴾ وَ ﴿هَلْ أَتَاكَ حَدِيْثُ الْغَاشِيَةِ﴾، فَإِذَا اجْتَمَعَ الْجُمُعَةُ وَالْعِيْدَانِ فِي يَوْمٍ قَرَأَ بِهِمَا.

'Allah's Messenger ﷺ would recite the chapter al-Aʿlā (87) and the chapter al-Ghāshiya (88) in (the two cycles of) ʿīd prayer even if the ʿīd day fell on a Friday.'[197]

Muʿāwiya ◌ asked Zayd b. Arqam ◌:

أَشَهِدْتَ مَعَ رَسُوْلِ اللهِ ﷺ عِيْدَيْنِ؟ قَالَ: نَعَمْ، صَلَّى الْعِيْدَيْنِ مِنْ أَوَّلِ النَّهَارِ، ثُمَّ رَخَّصَ فِي الْجُمُعَةِ.

If he had ever attended the two ʿīds (al-Fiṭr or al-Aḍḥā with Friday) with the Prophet ﷺ! He replied, 'Yes, he ﷺ offered the ʿīd prayer in the early morning and then permitted (those who were too distant from the city to obligate Friday prayer) to leave the Friday prayer.'[198]

About combining the two ʿīds in one day, Imam Muhammad writes in al-Jāmiʿ al-Ṣaghīr:

يَشْهَدُهُمَا جَمِيْعًا وَلَا يَتْرُكُ وَاحِدًا مِنْهُمَا، وَالْأُوْلَى مِنْهُمَا سُنَّةٌ وَالْأُخْرَى فَرِيْضَةٌ.

One must attend both of them and must not leave any of them, for the first one is (made imperative by) Sunna whereas the second one is an obligation.[199]

---

[197] Narrated by al-Nasāʾī in al-Sunan al-Kubrā, 1:547 §1775.
[198] Narrated by al-Nasāʾī in al-Sunan, 3:194 §1591.
[199] Ibn Nujaym al-Ḥanafī, al-Baḥr al-Rāʾiq, 2:70.

Al-Shāmī writes:

عِيْدَانِ اجْتَمَعَا فِي يَوْمٍ وَاحِدٍ، فَالْأَوَّلُ سُنَّةٌ وَالثَّانِي فَرِيْضَةٌ، وَلَا يُتْرَكُ وَاحِدٌ مِنْهُمَا.

> If two ʿīds fall on one and the same day, then the first one is (made imperative by) Sunna, whereas the second one is an obligation. Neither of the two must be missed.[200]

Imam Abū Bakr b. Masʿūd al-Kāsānī writes:

تَجِبُ صَلَاةُ الْعِيْدَيْنِ عَلَى أَهْلِ الْإِحْصَارِ كَمَا تَجِبُ الْجُمُعَةُ.

> The dwellers of a city are obligated to perform both the *ʿīds* (*al-Fiṭr* and *al-Aḍḥā*) like the obligation of Friday prayer.

He also comments upon the opinion of Imam Muhammad:

فَإِنَّهُ قَالَ فِي الْعِيْدَيْنِ اجْتَمَعَا فِي يَوْمٍ وَاحِدٍ، فَالْأَوَّلُ سُنَّةٌ ... فِي الْجَامِعِ الصَّغِيْرِ أَنَّهَا وَاجِبَةٌ بِالسُّنَّةِ ... وَالصَّحِيْحُ أَنَّهَا وَاجِبَةٌ.

> He (Imam Muhammad) said about the two *ʿīds* falling on one day that the first of them is Sunna ... in *al-Jāmiʿ al-Ṣaghīr* (it explains that it means) it is made imperative by Sunna ... so, the correct legal position would be that it is imperative.[201]

It is enough for us to know that our beloved Prophet ﷺ did perform both the *ʿīd* and Friday prayers. Our understanding of the matter is he allowed those from the outskirts of Medina to stay there and offer the Friday prayer if any of them wanted to, or to return home before

---

[200] Ibn ʿĀbidayn, *Radd al-Muḥtār*, 2: 166.

[201] Al-Kāsānī, *Badāʾiʿ al-Ṣānāʾiʿ*, 1:275.

offering Friday prayer if their houses were too distant to perform *ʿĪd* and Friday prayer. So, Friday prayer would be obligated upon those who would have remained there until the start of its time; and not upon those who would have left the city prior to that because being in the city is one of the conditions of its obligation.[202] [Allah ﷻ and His Messenger ﷺ know the best.]

Q.157. What is the difference between the Friday and *ʿĪd* prayers?

A: Both *ʿĪd* prayers are imperative but only upon those obligated to perform Friday prayers, with the same conditions as those of Friday. There are only two differences. Friday sermon is an essential condition for the validity of Friday prayer, so much so that the prayer without sermon is invalid, whereas it is Sunna for *ʿĪd* prayers and prayers without a sermon are valid although it is rendered reprehensible. The second difference regards the time of sermon, which is before the prayer in the case of Friday and after the prayer in the case of *ʿĪd*. If somebody delivers the sermon of *ʿĪd* prayer before the

---

[202] Our understanding of the matter is that there are two categories of people:

- Those who lived outside the city of Medina and their local population was too small to obligate *ʿĪd* or Friday prayer. They had the option to go back to their homes where Friday prayer won't be obligated or to stay in the city (in Medina in this case) where Friday prayer would be obligated (if they stayed there till the time that Friday prayer started). This is the reason the holy Prophet ﷺ permitted them to go home if they wanted to.
- Those who lived in the city (of Medina in this case) or wanted to stay there until the time that Friday Prayer would start. They did not have an option except to offer both the prayers to discharge their duty to Allah ﷻ.

prayer, it is reprehensible, but the prayer is done and it does not require redoing it.

Q.158. Is *ṣadaqa al-Fiṭr* imperative upon those who do not fast?

A: Fasting is not a condition for the obligation of *ṣadaqa al-Fiṭr*. If somebody was unable to fast for some excuse such as travel, illness or old age he still has to pay *ṣadaqa al-Fiṭr*. Even if somebody does not fast without any excuse (May Allah ﷻ save us from such exercise), *ṣadaqa al-Fiṭr* still behoves him.

Q.159. Can *ṣadaqa al-Fiṭr* be paid before the day of *ʿĪd*?

A: Yes, it can be. It is proven by the practice of Ibn ʿUmar ﷺ. Al-Nāfiʿ says:

كَانُوْا يُعْطُوْنَ قَبْلَ الْفِطْرِ بِيَوْمٍ أَوْ يَوْمَيْنِ.

> They (the Companions ﷺ) used to pay (*ṣadaqa al-Fiṭr*) a day or two prior to (the day of) *al-Fiṭr*.[203]

Q.160. Is *ṣadaqa al-Fiṭr* imperative upon a pre-pubescent?

A: Yes, it is. If he owns enough money, it will be paid from it. Or else, his parents or guardian will pay on his behalf.

Q.161. Who deserves to receive *ṣadaqa al-Fiṭr*?

A: They are same as the recipients of Zakat. If somebody does not deserve to receive Zakat, he does not deserve to

[203] Narrated by al-Bukhārī in *al-Ṣaḥīḥ*, 2:549 §1440.

receive *ṣadaqa al-Fiṭr* either. It is more fitting to choose the indigent and needy from amongst the recipients, to award *ṣadaqa al-Fiṭr* for the Prophet ﷺ said:

أَغْنُوْهُمْ فِي هَذَا الْيَوْمِ.

'Enrich them adequately on this day.'[204]

Q.162. Are we allowed to award *ṣadaqa al-Fiṭr* to our blood relations?

A: Yes, we are. We can award it to our relations such as brothers, sisters, uncle (both maternal and paternal), aunt etc. We cannot give it to our roots such as parents and grandparents or our branches such as our children and grandchildren. Likewise, a husband cannot give it to his wife or a wife to her husband.

Q.163. What amount is payable in *ṣadaqa al-Fiṭr* according to the Shariah?

A: It is about 2,045 grams of wheat or wheat-flour or 4,090 grams of dates or barley or its flour equivalent. It is more appropriate to give its price, for it is more useful to the needy. We can also pay the *ṣadaqa al-Fiṭr* of an entire family to one person.

---

[204] Narrated by al-Dāraquṭnī in *al-Sunan*, 2:152 §67.